Praise for
Be the Message

"This book will serve as a wake-up call for people everywhere to use their God-given talents to radically transform the community. Far too often there is a separation between the words that people speak and the actions that support them. We all have a unique calling on our lives, and we cannot reach our true potential until we learn to embrace that calling. I believe that God is raising a generation of believers who will be the hands and feet of Jesus, with a love so profound that the world cannot help but take notice. *Be the Message* is a guideline to living a Christ-centered life, not just in theory but through an all-consuming lifestyle of serving others. There is no limit to what the body of Christ can do when focused and motivated; our greatest days are ahead of us, if we would only learn to practice what we preach."

—MATTHEW BARNETT, senior pastor, Angelus Temple, Los
Angeles, and cofounder of The Dream Center

"Kerry and Chris Shook have an enthusiasm for authentic and active faith that is contagious. In a practical and straightforward style, this book tackles one of the most important theological distinctions of the Christian faith— the incarnation—and gives us real direction on how to live. I love it!"

—CHRIS SEAY, pastor, Ecclesia Church, Houston

"So much anxiety and stress in our lives is caused by the disconnect between our words and our walk. It's imperative for leaders to live authentic lives, in which the who and the what are congruent. Kerry and Chris Shook have given us a powerful biblical tool that will help you reduce that gap and truly come alive in your leadership and life."

—BRAD LOMENICK, key advisor, former president of Catalyst,
and author of *The Catalyst Leader*

"I love how God can take our greatest mess and turn it into our greatest message. *Be the Message* offers incredible hope and practical encouragement on how to let God work miracles in our lives."

    —NELSON SEARCY, lead pastor, The Journey Church,
      New York City

BOOKS BY KERRY AND CHRIS SHOOK

One Month to Live

One Month to Love

Be the Message

Be the Message

Taking Your Faith Beyond Words to a LIFE of ACTION

Kerry & Chris
SHOOK

Foreword by Rick Warren

WATERBROOK
PRESS

BE THE MESSAGE
PUBLISHED BY WATERBROOK PRESS
12265 Oracle Boulevard, Suite 200
Colorado Springs, Colorado 80921

All Scripture quotations, unless otherwise indicated, are taken from the Holy Bible, New International Version®, NIV®. Copyright © 1973, 1978, 1984, 2011 by Biblica Inc.™ Used by permission of Zondervan. All rights reserved worldwide. www.zondervan.com. Scripture quotations marked (CEV) are taken from the Contemporary English Version. Copyright © 1991, 1992, 1995 by American Bible Society. Used by permission. Scripture quotations marked (HCSB) are taken from the Holman Christian Standard Bible®, © copyright 1999, 2000, 2002, 2003, 2009 by Holman Bible Publishers. Used by permission. Scripture quotations marked (KJV) are taken from the King James Version. Scripture quotations marked (MSG) are taken from The Message by Eugene H. Peterson. Copyright © 1993, 1994, 1995, 1996, 2000, 2001, 2002. Used by permission of NavPress Publishing Group. All rights reserved. Scripture quotations marked (NASB) are taken from the New American Standard Bible®. © Copyright The Lockman Foundation 1960, 1962, 1963, 1968, 1971, 1972, 1973, 1975, 1977, 1995. Used by permission. (www.Lockman.org). Scripture quotations marked (NKJV) are taken from the New King James Version®. Copyright © 1982 by Thomas Nelson Inc. Used by permission. All rights reserved. Scripture quotations marked (NLT) are taken from the Holy Bible, New Living Translation, copyright © 1996, 2004, 2007. Used by permission of Tyndale House Publishers Inc., Carol Stream, Illinois 60188. All rights reserved. Scripture quotations marked (Phillips) are taken from The New Testament in Modern English, Revised Edition © 1972 by J. B. Phillips. Copyright renewed © 1986, 1988 by Vera M. Phillips.

Details in some anecdotes and stories have been changed to protect the identities of the persons involved.

Hardcover ISBN 978-1-4000-7381-8
eBook ISBN 978-0-307-72961-3

Cover design by Mark D. Ford

Published in the United States by WaterBrook Multnomah, an imprint of the Crown Publishing Group, a division of Random House LLC, New York, a Penguin Random House Company.

WATERBROOK and its deer colophon are registered trademarks of Random House LLC.

Library of Congress Cataloging-in-Publication Data
Shook, Kerry.
     Be the message : taking your faith beyond words to a life of action / Kerry and Chris Shook. — First
Edition.
          pages cm
     Includes bibliographical references
     ISBN 978-1-4000-7381-8 — ISBN 978-0-307-72961-3 (electronic) 1. Witness bearing (Christianity)
2. Christian life. I. Title.
     BV4520.S455 2014
     248.4—dc23

                                                                                      2014019700

Printed in the United States of America
2014—First Edition

10 9 8 7 6 5 4 3 2 1

SPECIAL SALES
Most WaterBrook Multnomah books are available at special quantity discounts when purchased in bulk by corporations, organizations, and special-interest groups. Custom imprinting or excerpting can also be done to fit special needs. For information, please e-mail SpecialMarkets@WaterBrookMultnomah.com or call 1-800-603-7051.

For Woodlands Church

*You have been God's message of grace to our family
every single day for the past twenty years.
We love you.*

Contents

Part 1: Transforming...
Your Words into a Life Message

Part 2: Discovering...
Your Unique Life Message

Part 3: Understanding...
The Message That Confounds the World

Contents

Part 4: Taking...
Your Life Message to the World Around You

Foreword

Hudson Taylor once said, "All God's giants have been weak people." My favorite example of a giant is Jacob. Jacob was a deceiver, a manipulator, and even a schemer. He spent much of his life scheming to get his way, making one mess after another. Then he'd run from it. This was the pattern of his life: create a mess and run.

Then one night Jacob had an encounter with God. He literally wrestled with God and said, "I'm not going to let go until you bless me, God." And God said, "Okay, I'll bless your life." The Lord grabbed Jacob's thigh and pulled his hip out of socket. He touched him. God touched him at a point of strength and turned it into a weakness. The Bible says that from that point on, Jacob's life was blessed, but he walked with a limp.

Kerry and Chris Shook know that instead of hiding and denying our weaknesses, we need to recognize them and learn from them. We need to learn to share them. We need to learn to glory in our weaknesses. If God is ever going to use us greatly, we'll walk with a limp the rest of our lives. We can hear about people's successes all day, and it will have absolutely no benefit to us. But when they start talking to us about their pain, all of a sudden they have our attention. Sharing our handicaps causes others to stop making excuses, to see the possibilities, and to rely on God.

If we're going to have a Christlike ministry, that means sometimes other people are going to find healing in the wounds in our lives.

In *Be the Message* Kerry and Chris have written a powerful guide on how to stop hiding behind our images so we can truly discover and live our authentic life message. This book is not for those who seek to be impressed;

it's for those who want to have an impact on the lives of others. We can impress people by talking about our successes, but we'll impact people when we admit our failures and weaknesses and point them to the God who can work a miracle out of our mess.

—Rick Warren
Pastor, Saddleback Church
Author, *The Purpose Driven Life*

Acknowledgments

We are so grateful to our children for, by God's grace, looking past all of the wrong messages we lived in front of them and seeing the right one, the only one that matters, the message of Jesus.

We could never thank the team from WaterBrook Multnomah enough. Steve Cobb, you always encourage us, and we are grateful for your friendship.

Thank you, Ken Petersen, for your tireless and brilliant work with us on the book. You brought out the best in us, and *Be the Message* wouldn't be what it is without your gifts and passion.

Thank you to Tom Winters for your commitment to our message, and a very special thanks to Orla Mathwig for your great work and patience every step of the way.

Thank you to the amazing staff at Woodlands Church for all you do each day in being the message of Christ to your families and thousands around the world.

Part 1

Transforming...

Your Words into a Life Message

We want you to know that, for us, this is more than another book and another message.

This is our personal journey of the past few years, a journey that has changed the way we think and the way we live.

It's truly been an awakening. We've become aware that the words we had been speaking, although true and biblical and well intended, were not always being acted out fully in our lives. We've been waking up to the real call of Christ, waking up to an understanding that the gospel is so much more than words spoken.

We're still on the path of this journey. We have a long way to go and much to learn. But we're discovering more each day.

God in His grace is already working. We see a difference in our family and church and community. We see needs met in people's lives all over the planet. And most of all, this experience of transforming words into life action has changed *us* in a deep and profound way.

In *Be the Message* we'll tell these amazing stories, take you with us on this eye-opening journey, and share with you what we've been learning.

1

As you read this book, understand that we are two people with one voice. We've found that when we work on a book together, it can be confusing to constantly identify who's speaking—Kerry or Chris. And so on these pages we've chosen to speak as one. Only when it's absolutely necessary to the meaning do we specify which one of us is writing. Of course, ministry for us has always been a shared calling, and so speaking as one voice accurately reflects who we are and what we do. But it's all the more appropriate for this book because we are living this new understanding of the gospel together.

And, wow, has it been an adventure! This illuminating, miraculous walk with Him has led us beyond words into greater authenticity and action.

We want this for you too. We challenge you to do more than just read this book. One of our key points, as you'll see, is to get beyond words, and so we don't want this to be just another book you read. We urge you to take these thoughts and discoveries and put them into action.

It all starts with a simple, fresh understanding about words and messages, life and calling, and the real meaning and purpose of the gospel.

I want to talk about God less
and walk with God more.
#BeTheMessage

The Great Disconnect

Preach the gospel at all times and when necessary use words.

St. Francis of Assisi

The Word became flesh—and then through theologians, it became words again.

Karl Barth

I'm sick of sermons. I'm tired of talking about God. I'm tired of hearing about God.

Now, that may seem strange to you. After all, I'm a pastor. I preach and teach. It's my job to talk about God. In many ways, my life is all about words and messages. It's what I've been gifted to do. It's been my vocation and calling.

But frankly, I'm tired of all the words. I'm tired of all the messages. I'm tired of hearing myself preach.

Don't get me wrong. I love the call that God has placed on my life, and I love teaching His life-changing Word. I still believe that there's deep value in all of that. But increasingly I'm feeling I talk so much about God that I sometimes fail to really experience Him. Sometimes my life seems more about words than it is about actions.

I want to talk about God less and walk with Him more.

I want to hear about God less and experience Him more.

The highway near our home is lined with more than our share of the nearly half-million billboards in the United States. As we drive past them, we can listen to our choice of the dozens of radio stations that fill the airwaves. Add to that another dozen broadcast television stations, hundreds of cable channels, Facebook posts, Twitter feeds, text messages, junk e-mail, and plain old-fashioned direct mail pouring into our mailboxes, and you see what I mean.

We're inundated with information. Our culture saturates us in a constant stream of daily messages that comes from every direction imaginable.

And the church is square in the middle of the problem, pumping out its own stream of information to help us increase our spiritual knowledge and become better Christians. There are 350,000 religious congregations in the United States, most of them with their own website. A quick check of Amazon.com as I'm writing this shows more than 159,000 Christian-living books, the precise category for this book.

That's a lot of sermons, Bible studies, podcasts, and audio files.

In the midst of all that noise, the Christian message often becomes just another slogan. It seems we've taken the disciples' experience of literally walking with Jesus, an experience lived out in the early church and divinely recorded and carefully handed down through the generations, and made it into nothing more than a sound bite. We've turned the inspired, life-giving Word into just one more set of words among many.

And we're party to it. We roll from sermon to sermon, Bible study to Bible study, event to event, striving to learn the language of faith—all with good intentions as we seek to be deepened and enriched spiritually. Yet so often it becomes just a rote exercise in saying the right things and giving the right answers. In doing so we reduce the gospel to a collection of tips and techniques, catchy phrases that show our mental agreement with certain philosophical and theological propositions, and a whole heap of pat answers.

We wind up with a lot of words and are quite separated from the actual experience of Jesus. For all those "spiritual" words, not much translates into how we live.

We've mastered messages. We haven't mastered life.

Hiding Behind the Words

This disconnect between message and life is something I experience as much as you do. It's something I've become more keenly, and more painfully, aware of in just the past few years.

As a pastor, I'm especially careful to make sure my life honors God, that my life in private matches my life in public. But there are other ways message and life get disconnected for me probably as much as they do for you.

For one, I have to admit that sometimes I hide behind the words I'm speaking. I notice this happens when I'm with someone who's in emotional or physical pain. I sometimes just don't know how to respond. There's an awkwardness in those moments, and to relieve the tension I find myself spouting the handy message, the Christian slogan about suffering, hope, and God's purposes—all true words, for sure, but words I'm actually hiding behind.

I too easily speak the sound-bite answer rather than live alongside someone in the painful question. Shouldn't I have the courage to sit without words beside that hurting soul?

Do you do this too? Give someone a message instead of your life? Do you find it easier to offer words instead of actions? Do you do as I do, often hide behind a nice-sounding message about someone's need rather than get your hands dirty in actually doing something to help?

It happens on a grander scale too.

I've realized my response to global problems and issues becomes just another set of words. They sometimes gush out of my mouth in the form of sound bites and statistics. I can say that of the 7 billion people on the planet, 1.4 billion live on less than $1.25 a day, 1.7 billion lack access to clean water, 35 million are living with HIV/AIDS, and 21,000 will die today of hunger or hunger-related causes.

All true, but the problem in saying this is that I'm hiding behind the message of the numbers. Sure, the numbers describe a real problem, but rattling them off is my way of sounding good while disconnecting that issue from my life. "The global problem is so big, and it needs to be addressed." And by saying those things I can sound like I'm really in the moment, really caring, really trying to change the world—all without being personally involved.

This changed for me when I read a news article about Stephen, a nine-year-old boy.

Stephen lived in a slum outside Kampala, Uganda. Orphaned and living on his own, he provided for himself by breaking rocks with a homemade hammer, working twelve hours every day in the scorching heat of the sun. Every twelve hours he managed to fill three five-gallon buckets with crushed rock. For all the dust and sweat, Stephen earned six cents per bucket, or eighteen cents for a day's work, which he used to buy food. After each excruciating day of backbreaking work, he spent the night alone in a mud hut.[1]

Now, this was just a news article on child labor, but it touched me personally. Reading about a real boy enduring hard labor couldn't help but affect me deeply. I thought about my own kids, about the children of other families I know. What if he were one of ours?

This was a wake-up call alerting me to the disconnect between my message and my life. Spouting facts and experiencing reality are two different things. I could look like a world changer without it really affecting my life. And that troubled me. How could there be such a gap between the desperate life of this child and the comfortable life I was able to have?

Yes, this was just a news article, but for me it became the beginning of more, something that would bridge the gap between my message and my life.

The Cost of Disconnection

I soon became aware of what the disparity between message and life does to my heart and soul.

Rick Warren has said the great disconnect between what we say we believe and how we really live causes most of the stress and discouragement in our lives.

I say that my health is very important, but I don't always eat right and exercise. I say that my family deserves top priority, but many times work and the so-called urgent demands of life crowd out family time. I say that God has first place in my life, but I rush into my busy schedule with just a quick prayer and a verse of the day rather than taking time to get quiet and sit still before the Creator of the universe. I say one thing, but I live something very different.

I say one thing but live another.

Sound familiar?

Such incongruity creates deep frustration and disappointment inside us.

The human heart cries out for an authentic life, a life that is outwardly consistent with the things we believe in our hearts and know to be true. But at the same time we're driven to achieve more, please others, and climb the ladder at work. In those frantic pursuits we proclaim messages we can't possibly live up to, and our authenticity is lost.

It works like this: In each arena of life, we want to be something, appear like something, attain something. We offer up a message (to others and ourselves) that creates an image or identity that helps us achieve what we want.

But there are two problems here.

One is that the image/identity we project in one arena might be completely different in another arena. So, to get ahead at work, we strive to be distant and disciplinary—yet at church we want to be considered caring and compassionate. Those two messages about ourselves don't fit together, and so we compartmentalize. We create different boxes with a separate identity for each arena of life.

We wind up with a work box, a recreation box, and a family-life box. We often add a Christian box for our life at church. We create boxes for convenience' sake, thinking it simply makes everything more manageable.

But before long those same boxes become traps. Rather than take us to a place of wholeness, those boxes fragment our lives. With that comes tension, stress, and frustration. No wonder we're so exhausted all the time!

Here's the other problem. Never mind the number of boxes. Even in just one box it's unlikely for the message we project to really match the person we truly are. Each message is what we *want* to be true about ourselves or want others to see about us in that box. But rarely does that message match the reality of our lives.

Deeper down, what we really long for is an authentic life, fully integrated in the present.

But along the way we become *dis*-integrated, our lives disconnected from the messages we project about ourselves. This message-life disconnect eats away at us inside.

A CHURCH OF DISCONNECTION

I can't talk about the great disconnect without talking about the church.

Know that I write these next words carefully and thoughtfully. I love the church and have devoted my life to serving the body of Christ. I also write these words humbly, because I know I have been guilty of some of the very things I'm about to describe.

But the truth is that many of us Christians in church have proclaimed words without following up with actions. We spend a lot of time talking, teaching, discussing, and arguing the Bible, but do we really live it out for the world to see? The world is tired of just hearing our sermons and Christian phrases; *they want to see a sermon lived out.* They quickly tune out our talk; they long to see the walk.

It's not that Bible studies, sermons, and church services aren't valuable. The talk is important for lots of reasons. But too often our words are just a form of posturing: how we project ourselves to be better or more spiritual than the next guy.

I think that's a big reason many people have the wrong idea of church. They think it's the place where perfect people meet up with other perfect people to sing about how perfect their lives are.

Nope.

The church is a place where sinners come together in their brokenness and acknowledge they're not who they might have claimed they were. Church is a place for people who admit they have fallen and have failed. It's a safe place to share our failures, our weaknesses, our addictions, our needs, and our pain.

It should be a place where we can be real, not cool.

As Craig Groeschel, pastor of LifeChurch, says, "Authenticity trumps cool every time."

By the way, when we pose and posture with messages that are disconnected from the reality of our lives as sinners, you know what gets created?

Religion.

That's why outsiders consider *religion* such a bad word. They recognize the huge gap between the words of Christians and their actual lives. And that disconnect gets labeled with the word *hypocrisy.* The reason so many are quick to launch the *h* word at people in the church is that our words don't match our actions.

In fact, it's this lack of authenticity that is driving so many young people away from the church. As Dave Kinnaman said in his book *unChristian: What a New Generation Really Thinks About Christianity...and Why It Matters,* "When outsiders...see Christians not acting like Jesus, they quickly conclude that the group deserves an unChristian label. Like a corrupted computer file or a bad photocopy, Christianity, they say, is no longer in pure form, and so they reject it. One quarter of outsiders say that their foremost perception of Christianity is that the faith has changed for the worse. It has gotten off track and is not what Christ intended. *Modern-day Christianity no longer seems Christian.*"[2]

I believe the church God intended is not supposed to be about religion. It's all about restoring broken lives.

If only we would talk less and walk with God more.

WORDS AND THE WORD

Another thing.

All these words can increase our knowledge, but only the Word—Jesus Christ—can change our lives. Christianity is not a slogan, a sound bite, or even a sermon. It's a personal relationship with the Savior, a relationship that plays out in our daily lives. We are called to emulate Jesus's life, not by parroting Bible verses and using hip religious language, but by living the gospel through our lives, making it real in our actions.

In fact, the great disconnect was precisely the focus of much of Jesus's ministry. In particular it came up repeatedly in His run-ins with the religious leaders of the day, the Pharisees. We might think of the Pharisees as the masters of legalism in the church of that time. They were sticklers for saying all the right things, and they were the ultimate posers of proper religion.

In one encounter Jesus said to the Pharisees point-blank, "You study the Scriptures diligently because you think that in them you have eternal life. These are the very Scriptures that testify about me, yet you refuse to come to me to have life" (John 5:39–40).

Really, it's pretty comical. The Pharisees had their heads buried in the Scriptures, the sacred rules and regulations, the words of religion. Meanwhile they were completely oblivious to the Word, Jesus, standing right before them.

The Pharisees talked about the life of faith, but they reduced it to mere religion, belief confined to words alone. Legalism. They prized the use of the correct language but avoided the lifestyle of faith by every means possible. *They talked about faith but stripped it of life.*

Isn't that the problem we feel? Isn't that part of the disconnect? Life can be filled with sermons but empty of life.

I think it's interesting that the "sermon" Jesus Himself is best known for, the Sermon on the Mount, isn't a sermon in any conventional sense. In fact, you could call it the antisermon. It's brilliant, a message that dismantles all the standard messages that people, and especially the Pharisees, were using at the time.

Given on the side of a mountain in front of a large crowd, the Sermon on the Mount was the launch party for Jesus's ministry. Jesus delivered the speech that tells everyone that authenticity matters, that their message needs to be lived out in their lives.

I encourage you to read the Sermon on the Mount (Matthew 5–7), especially with the great disconnect in mind. Notice how often the word *hypocrite* is used. Jesus is speaking directly to those whose words are not lived out in their actions. And when Jesus repeatedly uses the phrase "You have heard that it was said," He's calling out the common messages and sermons that were spoken and preached at the time.

Take a closer look: "You have heard that it was said, 'Eye for eye, and tooth for tooth.' But I tell you, do not resist an evil person. If anyone slaps you on the right cheek, turn to them the other cheek also" (5:38–39). The Pharisees' common sermon of the day was the letter of the law: "eye for eye…" But Jesus surprises everyone by turning that on its head. He calls people to act— live—differently from what was expected: "Turn to them the other cheek also."

Oswald Chambers wrote, "The teaching of the Sermon on the Mount is not, 'Do your duty,' but is, in effect, 'Do what is not your duty.' It is not your duty to go the second mile, or to turn the other cheek, but Jesus said that if we are His disciples, we will always do these things.… Never look for right-eousness in the other person, but never cease to be righteous yourself. We are always looking for justice, yet the essence of the teaching of the Sermon on the Mount is—Never look for justice, but never cease to give it."[3]

You see, Jesus consistently challenged the religious sermonizing of His world, calling people to go beyond words and live in a radically different and authentic way.

The problem of your life and mine is the disparity between the messages we proclaim and the lives we actually lead. And Jesus is telling us, just as He told the Pharisees, to talk a lot less and follow Him more. He's calling us to lift our heads from the noise of the words on the page and to look at Him, the living Word.

He's daring us to live lives consistent with who we are and what God calls us to do.

This is the adventure of being the message.

Hear God's Voice, Obey God's Call

As you walk this path, I want to share with you some practical tools I have found to be helpful. At the end of each chapter are two application sections: "The Divine Whisper" and "Love the One in Front of You."

One of the things I've had to learn along the journey is, quite frankly, to shut up. Shut up and listen to God. I have discovered that we have to stop talking long enough to hear God's divine whisper.

The account of the prophet Elijah in the Old Testament has a great lesson for us. When Elijah needed clarity from God, he cried out to the Lord. But God didn't come in a way Elijah expected: "The LORD said, 'Go out and stand on the mountain in the presence of the LORD, for the LORD is about to pass by.' Then a great and powerful wind tore the mountains apart and shattered the rocks before the LORD, but the LORD was not in the wind. After the wind there was an earthquake, but the LORD was not in the earthquake. After the earthquake came a fire, but the LORD was not in the fire. And after the fire came a gentle whisper" (1 Kings 19:11–12).

I love that phrase "a gentle whisper." God speaks to us through a gentle whisper in our hearts. The problem is that too often we're talking and not listening. The section "The Divine Whisper" at the end of each chapter is designed to help you carve out a time of quiet and listening.

Another lesson I've learned is that merely understanding God's call to be the message is not enough. The whole point is to change words into actions! And so we need to find ways of acting on God's call, right now.

But sometimes we shrink from the call to action because we feel we need to do something big or substantial or global. Yet God never asks us to do something big for Him. He asks us to take small steps of faith so He can do something big in us and through us.

The section "Love the One in Front of You" at the end of each chapter is designed to help you focus on the one small thing you can do right now.

Let's take a step of faith and let God lead us on the great adventure of being the message and living the gospel. As we let God do something great and profound *inside* of us, we will begin to see God do something great and profound *outside* of us.

The Divine Whisper

1. Read Psalm 46:10 out loud: "He says, 'Be still, and know that I am God; I will be exalted among the nations, I will be exalted in the earth.'"
2. Read it again, silently. Pray. Ask God to open your heart to hear His "gentle whisper."
3. Take a deep breath and realize that He's God and you're not. Just relax in the Lord and remember that His purpose will be accomplished in the world and in your life.
4. Spend five minutes in silence before God, allowing Him to restore your soul. This practice may feel uncomfortable at first. Five minutes may feel like an hour. But you have to detox from noise addiction so you can hear the divine whisper of God.

Love the One in Front of You

1. Pick someone you see regularly but may not know well (for example, your child's teacher, a coworker, the custodian), and look for practical ways to brighten that person's day.
2. Reread the statistics of global suffering in chapter 1. Ask God to open your heart to the fact that all pain is personal. Each statistic is made up of real individuals. Try to imagine a living, breathing person as one of those statistics.
3. Invite a friend to read *Be the Message* with you. Together, go on the journey to talk less about God and walk with Him more.

Your image may communicate
a brand, but your life shouts
the real message.
#BeTheMessage

2

Every Life Shouts

*Actions speak louder than words but not nearly
as often.*

Mark Twain

*People may doubt what you say, but they will
always believe what you do.*

Lewis Cass

Your life is a message. My life is a message. Whether we're Christian or
not, we convey a message to those around us simply by the way we live.
It's a message that our friends and family hear loud and clear. It's a message
that strangers can see from afar. It's a message that comes from the core of
who we are, expressed through the everyday actions we take and choices we
make.

Every life shouts.

Today the business world emphasizes branding, the image portrayed
by a business or product that distinguishes it from others in the same field.
That word, *brand,* is sometimes used to describe people as well. Of course,
celebrities have a brand identity that they take great pains to shape and

protect, but in a way *every* person has a brand. Your brand is the image of yourself you attempt to portray publicly.

In 2005 Lance Armstrong stood at the top of the bike-racing world. He had won the Tour de France an astounding seven consecutive times, and he had overcome testicular cancer that at one point had spread to various parts of his body. Armstrong cultivated himself as a brand that projected the image of a super athlete with great physical stamina, a medical miracle. His brand had been picked up by more than half a dozen companies, including Nike, RadioShack, and bicycle maker Trek.

But then Armstrong's real life started to shout. What emerged were allegations of doping. For a while Armstrong managed the accusations and protected his brand. But eventually the truth of his life—that he had cheated, that he had doped, that he had lied to everyone—pierced through the public brand image he'd so carefully cultivated. In 2012, Armstrong was stripped of his cycling titles, and his sponsors dropped him.

His life spoke the truth and toppled his brand.

Ultimately a life message shouts more clearly and loudly than a brand message. Your image may communicate an outward brand, but your life shouts the real inner message.

The movie *Frost/Nixon* tells the true story of one of the most famous interviews in American political history, between British TV celebrity David Frost and president Richard Nixon. The interviews occurred after Nixon had resigned and left the White House, but at the time he was still maintaining his innocence of the Watergate cover-up.

What's interesting is that the event presented two men who were each working on their brand image: Nixon trying to protect and ensure his presidential legacy, and Frost trying to overcome his lightweight image through a substantive news story.

The series of interviews culminates in a climactic final session where

Frost induces Nixon to blurt out the revealing statement "When the president does it, that means it's not illegal." In that momentous sentence the truth inside Nixon shouted, eventually leading to his confession of his participation in the Watergate cover-up.

Nixon had run for office as a "law and order" candidate. Yet when his own people broke the law, he lied to cover it up and went to great lengths to keep the truth a secret. That crisis rocked the nation to its foundation and gave us a prime example of someone who talked one way while living another.

We've become practically numb to reports of hypocrisy. Politicians say what everyone wants to hear, whether it's true or not, in order to push a policy through or to get elected. Every few months, it seems, we hear of people in the public eye who promote traditional values and love of family while being involved in adulterous affairs.

You may not have a national stage or media platform, but you do have a public image to the people around you: your family, kids, parents, friends, co-workers. That public image is a kind of brand that you project and cultivate.

Unfortunately, most of us spend more time on our outward brand image than we do on our inner life message.

The truth is that your actions tell the real story of what's inside you. They shout so loud they drown out any attempts to control your image. This is why Armstrong and Nixon, whose brand images were quite different from who they really were deep inside, couldn't sustain the illusion of authenticity.

At some point, the real you makes itself known.

Actions Yell Louder Than Words

Some of the messages that our lives convey reflect habits we indulge in, things we do in secret that we think no one sees, or even not-so-secret habits that plague our lives.

Pete lived with his wife and infant daughter in the Bronx section of New York City. They went out for a walk one day, Pete pushing the stroller with his wife by his side. On most days, even in a crowded urban environment, that would be a picturesque scene—husband, wife, and baby spending time together amid the bustle of the big city—but Pete had a problem. He was addicted to heroin, and it had been too long since his last fix.

Not far from their apartment they came to a pawn shop. By then Pete's need for drugs was overwhelming. Desperate to satisfy his body's craving, he lifted his daughter from the stroller, handed her to his wife, and pushed the stroller into the pawn shop, where he pawned it for cash to purchase drugs.

Pete sent a message to his wife that day: that his needs were paramount; that nothing about their life together was sacred, stable, or secure; that he would do anything to maintain his drug habit. That message can shake a person and a marriage to the core.

Life messages sent.

Life messages received.

Drug addiction, sexual abuse, uncontrolled anger, pride, insecurity, and dozens of other issues have etched indelible scars on our characters and personalities, both as the offenders and the offended. If you're one who has been through that, you know the messages that have been written on your life, some of them carved there by you and some by others. And whether we've personally wrestled with those problems or not, we've all seen instances of them in families and individuals we know and love.

Life is messy. Some of it is a mess others made for us, but a lot of it is a mess we've made for ourselves, sometimes in seemingly insignificant ways.

April had a three-year-old son who participated in a mother's-day-out program at their church. One day April arrived at the church to pick up her son and was called aside by one of the workers. Quietly, she told April that her son had used inappropriate language that day. "Totally in the correct context," the worker grinned good-naturedly, "but inappropriate."

April was worried and asked what happened. "He was playing with a toy and couldn't get it to fit together properly," the worker explained. "He tried several times, but he couldn't get it to work right. Then he stomped his little foot and muttered a profanity under his breath."

The mother's-day-out worker couldn't keep a straight face when she talked about it, but April was totally embarrassed. Not only because of her son's profanity but because she knew where he heard it—at home—and she knew the person he'd heard it from—her. But until that moment she hadn't realized she was being that obvious about her choice of language or that her son was listening that closely.

Our life choices shout a message to those around us.

Recently a friend told me about his father-in-law, who is an ordained denominational minister and licensed psychologist. He spent his adult life in ministry and education, both as a military chaplain and as a civilian pastor and educator. Highly educated, he holds two bachelor's degrees, three master's degrees, and two PhDs. That's a lot of education! Of the people in the United States who are twenty-five years or older, only about 1 percent have even a single PhD. This guy has two.

Certain choices the father-in-law made when his children were young led to contentious relationships with them, much of which remains unresolved even today. Even with that, all his children grew up to obtain postgraduate degrees, and two have PhDs. Both sons-in-law and his daughter-in-law have postgraduate degrees. And all of his children work in education or ministry. In spite of the childhood trauma, arguments, and tension, he communicated to them the message that education mattered more than anything.

They heard that message because it was the message he lived. They heard it, applied it to their own lives, and passed that message to their children. It carried across all the clutter and confusion in their lives, above everything else that was said, past all the wrongly guided decisions, because it was the one message that was clearly and consistently lived before them.

The messages we communicate by our lifestyles are the most powerful messages we send. People are watching and listening. Not to the messages we wish we could give, but to the ones we can't help but give—what we show them by the way we conduct our everyday lives.

Nowhere is this more true than in parenting. And it never shows up simply as a one-to-one transference: you like sports so your kids do too, or you like to do creative things and so do they. Instead, it appears dynamically and exponentially. The father who allows himself a drink every evening gets a call in the night from the police informing him that his son has been arrested for DUI. The mother who's obsessed with her appearance learns her daughter has been struggling with an eating disorder.

The life you choose and try to hide will become a life that shouts. Who you are will emerge at some point. That will be your message to the world.

A Life Message Close to Home

The message of this book is personal. And I've never been more aware of how my life message shouted than when I saw it reflected back to me in the eyes of our children.

Before we had kids, I could easily fool myself into thinking I was always practicing what I preached. But children, especially teenagers, completely destroy any false images you have of yourself. Kids have a sensitive hypocrisy detector that even spiritual pride can't fool.

Our children, now in their late teens and early twenties, used to quickly let me know when I lapsed into saying one thing while doing another. I would be driving down the street, intent on getting to our destination, and one of our sons would say, "You didn't come to a complete stop at that stop sign like you always tell me to do." Or "You're going fifteen miles per hour over the speed limit, and you warned me just yesterday about the consequences of speeding."

We laugh about the hypocrisy detectors our kids have that catch us in the act of exhibiting an integrity gap, but many of the unintended messages we send can hurt deeply.

Christmas is a fun time at our house. No matter where we go or what we're doing through the year, everyone seems to get back home for the holidays. A few years ago our oldest children, who'd been away at college, were back home. Everyone was together again like it used to be. We spent some great time as a family, going out for dinner or coffee and just hanging out. But as Christmas week drew near, we had to get ready for services at church.

When I (Kerry) work on a sermon, I sometimes zone in on the message and zone out on everything else. So I was at my desk, focused on finishing the message for our Christmas Eve service, when one of our sons came into the study and casually said, "Hey, Dad. How's it going?"

Without looking up I said, "Oh, it's going great." My eyes were glued to my work, and my voice had a detached tone. He lingered a moment near the desk, then drifted out of the room. I didn't think much of it.

The next day we were driving up to church for the Christmas Eve service rehearsal. The service was later that evening, and this was our final opportunity to get everything just right. As usual, I was running late and in a rush. My son was in the car with me, and somewhere between our house and the church he said, "Dad, I've got to tell you something that's on my mind."

"Sure," I replied, once again not really giving him my full attention.

"Yesterday when I came in the study and you were working on the message and I said, 'Dad, how's it going,' you didn't even look up. You were just so into it. You didn't even stop, and it makes me feel unimportant when you do that. It makes me feel like you care more about church and work than you do about me."

That got my attention, but rather than addressing the issue, I became defensive. "What do you mean?" I said. "I had to spend time finishing up my message right then."

"I know," he said. "I get all that, Dad. You're the greatest, and you've been there for me, but sometimes, you know, when you are really into something, you don't stop even for a moment, and it's like your family is not important enough for you to stop and connect." By then he'd lowered his voice.

He added quietly, "I just don't want to settle for that in my relationship with you."

In an instant I saw our children when they were much younger, tugging on my leg as I was talking to someone, or trying to get on my lap as I was working on a sermon, or trying to get my attention while I was talking on the telephone. And I heard myself say, "Just a minute. I'll be... Just hold on... Just hold on... I'll be right there. Just hold on..."

Then the thoughts came flooding in. *They're older now. Those moments are gone, and they're never coming back, and...* Tears welled up in my eyes. I tried to hold them back but they were coming, and there was nothing I could do about it.

My life message had shouted to my son during my distractedness. It said that a church service was more important to me than my son.

Now, look, I get that we have urgencies in our lives every day. Things distract us. Things call out to us to be handled. The issue isn't that we all have jobs to perform and details of life to take care of. It's the pattern of behaviors that our lives become devoted to.

I knew it wasn't just about the Christmas Eve service. It was about how my life was saying that work was more important than my family. It was another wake-up call for me.

It was time for me to look at my own life message and what it was shouting to my family.

THE LIFE MESSAGE YOU CHOOSE TO LIVE

Regardless of the circumstances of your past, you get to choose today what your life message to the world will be. Regardless of the sins and mistakes of your past, because of God's grace, the rest of your story has yet to be written.

Maybe this passage in Isaiah is exactly what you need today to remind you that God can rewrite your life message: "Forget the former things; do not dwell on the past. See, I am doing a new thing! Now it springs up; do you not perceive it? I am making a way in the wilderness and streams in the wasteland" (43:18–19).

I encourage you to examine the message your life has been demonstrating. If the message falls short of the words you are speaking, ask God for His grace and forgiveness, and let Christ have the pen to write a new story for you from now on.

Your public brand isn't ultimately going to hold up unless it mirrors your private reality. As we've seen from celebrities and politicians, you can't maintain a public image that is at odds with your inner self. What's inside you will eventually demonstrate to the world who you really are. Choosing your life message requires you to live intentionally, consciously working to make sure that what you say and what you project reflect who you really are deep down inside.

So what do you want your life message to be?

The Divine Whisper

1. Read Jeremiah 33:3 out loud: "Call to me and I will answer you and tell you great and unsearchable things you do not know."
2. Read that verse again silently. Ask God to show you "great and unsearchable things you do not know."
3. Spend five minutes in silence thanking God for what you have and trusting Him for what you need.

Love the One in Front of You

1. Write down the names of three people who are very close to you. Pray for them today, asking God for wisdom and guidance in knowing how to be a blessing in their lives.
2. Actively do something to encourage one of those three people. Ask God to give you a creative idea. No matter how small or insignificant it might seem to you, a small act of kindness can speak volumes to someone else.

Before you open your mouth to
speak, open your heart to care.

#BeTheMessage

3

You Are the Gospel

*The "Gospel" is not a sermon title or the name
of a book in the Bible. The Gospel is the person
of Jesus Christ and it is the power of God to bring
people to salvation.*

John Paul Warren

*The Word became flesh and blood, and moved
into the neighborhood.*

John 1:14, MSG

A great place to begin your journey toward being the message is to read
the gospel of John.

If you have never read it, it's an ideal place to start exploring the Bible. If
you've read the book of John many times before and feel as if you've "been
there, done that," be prepared for God to shake you up and open your eyes
to see something brand-new in this familiar passage.

God gets our attention in the very first verse: "In the beginning was the
Word, and the Word was with God, and the Word was God." John is laying

it out simply and directly: if you were wondering who Jesus is, look no further. John uses the term "the Word" as a clear reference to Jesus Christ. Jesus was with God the Father at the creation of the world and is God Himself.

Jesus is the Word. The message—the gospel—is the person of Jesus.

For all the words and sermons and Bible studies we absorb, for all the theology we argue, for all the Christian books we read, it's actually pretty simple. The gospel message is not about millions of words and sermons and books. The message is about one life. One person. The life, the reality of Jesus Christ.

Once you realize that, it will radically change the way you read your Bible. You see, the purpose of reading it isn't to know the Bible better; the purpose is to know *Jesus* better. We study Scripture not to increase our biblical knowledge but to grow closer to Christ. The late Bible professor Howard Hendricks put it this way: "The Bible was written not to satisfy your curiosity but to help you conform to Christ's image."

To help you remember to experience the reality of Jesus's life, try pulling an empty chair next to you during your daily Bible reading. Imagine for a moment that Christ is sitting in that chair. Of course, He is next to you all the time, but having the empty chair beside you may help you focus on His presence and remind you that Jesus Christ is with you as you read.

It's incredible! We not only have the book but the author of the book, the Word Himself, right there to help us understand what it means.

Suddenly the words aren't just words. They are *the* Word, Jesus Himself, His life.

ANOTHER DISCOVERY

But that's just the beginning. Another insight becomes clear as we reflect on the history of the early church and the lives of those Jesus walked with.

Something gets lost as we read the Bible today, especially the New Testament, and engage with the writings of the apostles: Paul's letters, those of Peter and John, and Luke's account of the early church in the book of Acts. We in the twenty-first century have the benefit of all these letters and writings; this is the Holy Bible we read and study. It has become core to our faith.

But Christians in the early church didn't have the full collection of inspired scriptures we have. The Bible as we know it was not yet written, much less collected into the set of books and epistles we have now. History tells us that most of the New Testament books weren't written until decades after Jesus died and ascended into heaven. Paul's letters weren't widely circulated until the end of the first century. Before that, the church in Ephesus, say, would certainly have received the letter Paul wrote to them that we now know as Ephesians, but they wouldn't necessarily yet have knowledge of the letter to the Colossians or the Philippians or other churches.

The full Bible, in fact, was not totally set and approved by the church until some four hundred years after Christ.

So what did the early Christians do before they had these written messages? before they had the Bible books? before they had the New Testament?

They had the life of Jesus.

There's a very interesting, often-overlooked fact in the book of Acts about the disciples after Christ ascended into heaven. They were down to eleven disciples from the original twelve (remember Judas, who betrayed Jesus, hanged himself). The eleven believed they needed to replace Judas. They said, "It is necessary to choose one of the men who have been with us the whole time the Lord Jesus was living among us, beginning from John's baptism to the time when Jesus was taken up from us. For one of these must become a witness with us of his resurrection" (1:21–22).

In short, they knew it was important to elect a twelfth man with the right credentials. The requirement was that he needed to be someone who knew Jesus personally, who had walked with Him through His ministry from baptism through ascension. They needed someone who, like the other eleven, was a witness to the life of Christ.

They needed someone who could carry a firsthand testimony to others. The next verses explain that the man chosen was Matthias, who had been with Jesus throughout His entire earthly ministry. The disciples were to carry the life message of Jesus, *based on knowing Jesus personally.*

Maybe you've read about the disciples all your life and are tempted to skim over this point. Don't miss this. I encourage you to let this truth hit you in a fresh way. The disciples were very conscious of the fact that their calling was based on their personal connection with Jesus. They knew they were witnesses to the Son of God on earth. They understood that *Jesus's life was the message,* and they were to carry it into the world. As John would later write, "We observed His glory, the glory as the One and Only Son from the Father, full of grace and truth" (John 1:14, HCSB).

Long before there was a New Testament, the disciples knew what the gospel was—Jesus's life—and they understood that as witnesses to that life, they carried that life message, that gospel, that "good news," to everyone they encountered. This had nothing to do with words on a page, but it was all about experiencing "the Word" in life.

So, when Jesus said before His return to heaven, "Go into all the world and preach the gospel to all creation" (Mark 16:15), He wasn't talking about preaching sermons on the books of the Bible or doing studies on the New Testament epistles. They hadn't been written yet.

No, He was talking about giving testimony to what they had seen: His life, His death, His resurrection.

Jesus in Every Book

Now, again I want to be clear about what I mean here. I'm not saying that Bible reading or Bible study is irrelevant. Not at all. In fact, the reason I believe the words in the Bible are true and life changing is because Jesus, the Word, is alive in every word.

In fact, Jesus Christ is mentioned in every book of the Bible, including those in the Old Testament. It's His story from beginning to end.

In Genesis, He is the Light of the World, the Creator
of all things.

In Exodus, He is the Passover Lamb that delivers His
children.

In Leviticus, He is the High Priest who bridges the
gap between God and man.

In Numbers, He is the Cloud and the Fire that lead
the people through the desert.

In Deuteronomy, He is the Prevailing Prophet.

In Joshua, He is the Captain of our salvation.

In Judges, He is the Great Judge of the living and the
dead.

In Ruth, He is the Kinsman-Redeemer who redeems
the lost and the lonely.

In 1 and 2 Samuel, He is the Voice of Truth in the
middle of the night.

In 1 and 2 Kings, He is the One True King.

In 1 and 2 Chronicles, He is the Holy One.

In Ezra, He is the Faithful One.

In Nehemiah, He is the Rebuilder of broken walls.

In Esther, He is the Rescuer in the time of need.

In Job, He is the Restorer of all things, the Maker of
all things new.

In Psalms, He is the Great Shepherd.

In Proverbs and Ecclesiastes, He is the Wisdom of God.

In the Song of Solomon, He is the Banner of unconditional love that is over us.

In Isaiah, He is the Suffering Servant.

In Jeremiah and Lamentations, He is the God whose
heart breaks for us.

In Ezekiel, He is the Resurrection and the Life to dry
bones.

In Daniel, He is the Son of Man coming in the clouds.

In Hosea, He is the Bridegroom who never stops
loving.

In Joel, He is the Salvation for all.

In Amos, He is the Burden Bearer and the Load
Lifter.

In Obadiah, He is the Mighty Savior.

In Jonah, He is the God of the second chance.

In Micah, He is the Messenger of good news.

In Nahum, He is the Restorer of justice.

In Habakkuk, He is the Interceder for the broken.

In Zephaniah, He is Strength for the weak and the
helpless.

In Haggai, He is the Cleansing Fountain.

In Zechariah, He is the pierced Son of God.

In Malachi, He is the Son of Righteousness.

In Matthew, He is the Messiah and the Friend of
sinners.
In Mark, He is the Miracle Worker.
In Luke, He is the Son of Man.
In John, He is the Son of God.
In Acts, He is the Power of God.
In Romans, He is the Gift of salvation.
In 1 and 2 Corinthians, He is the Last Adam who
reverses all wrongs.
In Galatians, He is all Freedom.
In Ephesians, He is the Cornerstone that the builders
rejected, but He is now the Chief Cornerstone
on which all life is built.
In Philippians, He is the Name Above All Names
who meets our every need.
In Colossians, He is the Fullness of God, the Hope
of glory.
In 1 and 2 Thessalonians, He is the Peace of God.
In 1 and 2 Timothy, He is the Great Mediator
between God and man.
In Titus, He is our Blessed Hope.
In Philemon, He is the Friend who sticks closer than
any brother.
In Hebrews, He is the Blood that washes away all
sin.
In James, He is the Great Physician.
In 1 and 2 Peter, He is the Great Shepherd.
In 1, 2, and 3 John, He is Everlasting Love.
In Jude, He is the God who saves us.

In Revelation, He is the Alpha and the Omega, the
      Beginning and the End, the First and the
      Last; the Bright and Morning Star; the Lion
      of Judah; the Returning King of kings and
      Lord of lords.

From Genesis to Revelation, Jesus is our hope, the gospel thread that runs from Genesis to Revelation. The Word, Jesus Christ, is alive in every word on every page of the Bible.

Christianity is all about the message embodied in the life of Jesus Christ. As Peter said, "God has raised this Jesus to life, and we are all witnesses of it" (Acts 2:32).

Two thousand years ago the disciples went to the corners of the known world and told people about Jesus's life. They talked about what they'd seen—the miracles Jesus performed, the people He raised from the dead. They said that they saw Him die and saw Him walking with them after He rose from the dead.

Today we are called to the corners of our world to do the same thing. We weren't alive when Jesus walked the earth, but we have the witness of His life message through those disciples, and those they talked to, and those that those people talked to, and on and on. The church is the passing down of that witness through the generations.

But we also have another kind of witness, that of Jesus Christ working in our own lives. Yes, He turned the water into wine in His ministry on earth, but He has also transformed us into something beautiful through His ministry in our lives today.

Jesus's life message is the gospel.

And we are the witnesses to that life message today.

PUTTING TWO AND TWO (AND TWO) TOGETHER

There's one more piece of the puzzle we need to examine.

Jesus told His disciples, "Before long, the world will not see me anymore, but you will see me. Because I live, you also will live. On that day you will realize that I am in my Father, and you are in me, and I am in you" (John 14:19–20).

"I am in you." Did you get the power of that statement?

Take a look at this passage in Colossians: "The mystery that has been kept hidden for ages and generations, but is now disclosed to the Lord's people. To them God has chosen to make known among the Gentiles the glorious riches of this mystery, which is Christ in you, the hope of glory" (1:26–27). The apostle Paul didn't say, "Christ and you." He said, "Christ in you."

When you wake up to the fact that a lot of the Bible talks about Christ *in* us, verses start popping out at you from the pages of the Bible:

Romans 8:11: "And if the Spirit of him who raised Jesus from the dead is living in you, he who raised Christ from the dead will also give life to your mortal bodies because of his Spirit who lives in you."

Ephesians 2:22: "And in him you too are being built together to become a dwelling in which God lives by his Spirit."

1 John 2:14: "I write to you, dear children, because you know the Father. I write to you, fathers, because you know him who is from the beginning. I write to you, young men, because you are strong, and the word of God lives in you, and you have overcome the evil one."

That phrase really jumps out: "The word of God lives in you."

So let's put two and two and two together.

Jesus is the Word. The Word is the gospel. Christ, the Word, lives in you.

Translation: *You are the gospel.*

Wow.

Two plus two plus two equals…amazing.

And suddenly that verse from Corinthians means so much more: "You are a letter from Christ, the result of our ministry, written not with ink but with the Spirit of the living God, not on tablets of stone but on tablets of human hearts" (2 Corinthians 3:3).

Friend, you and I are the gospel.

Making It Personal

I'm a pastor. I should know this stuff, right? But the truth is, I'm just like you, figuring things out as I live my life. Once this simple understanding—that I am the gospel—became real to me, it changed my life. Or, I should say, *is* changing my life; it's a process that's still working inside me every day.

One immediate change was that in my reading of the Bible, familiar passages suddenly took on new meaning. In fact, so much in Scripture makes sense now, like jigsaw pieces falling into perfect place, constructing a picture. This deeper understanding of God's purpose wasn't about words but about people. Not a message but a life.

My life. Your life.

This becomes our life message: that we are the embodiment of the gospel to the world. Once we grasp this, the entire focus of our lives changes.

We talked before about those boxes we find ourselves in and the stress that comes from maintaining different identities in different areas of our lives. Well, when we truly realize that Christ in us is the gospel, that our purpose is to be the gospel to others, all this fragmentation diminishes. We have one focus, one purpose, and we find ourselves becoming whole again.

Now, I'm not saying that I don't still struggle with that. My life can get hectic. But more and more I am finding that my life has greater unity and definition because now only one thing matters.

By focusing our lives on Him and by allowing Him to live through us, we move away from a life of separate identities to one with a single identity that is rooted and grounded in Him.

Being the gospel becomes the simple laser-beam focus of our lives.

Hands and Feet

Perhaps the biggest change I've experienced from my journey has been a new understanding of the church. When you begin to understand that you are the message, you will come to see the church in a whole new way.

The truth is that the church is not about religion, at least as most people think of religion. It's not about empty rituals or routine practices and observances.

The role of the church isn't even just about teaching, preaching, and communicating messages and words about the gospel.

The church is so much more than words; the church is the gospel lived out in community.

As we each have Christ in us and each have our own life message that's intertwined with the life message of Jesus Christ, the church becomes a community of people who live out the gospel not just in the church building but in the larger community and around the world.

But I think we develop in church the idea that "the gospel is spoken here," meaning that we kind of contain the gospel within our walls. That your church or my church is where the gospel happens. That the church building is the chief place to experience the message of Christ. Well, the church is one place it happens, but if we think the gospel can be contained within the church's walls, we've missed the point.

We are the gospel, and everything we do should reflect that message to those around us. We have personally become His witnesses to the world. You and I have become the hands and feet of Jesus just as the disciples were after He returned to heaven.

In his book *Radical,* David Platt wrote, "If we were left to ourselves with the task of taking the gospel to the world, we would immediately begin planning innovative strategies and plotting elaborate schemes. We would organize conventions, develop programs, and create foundations.... But Jesus is so different from us. With the task of taking the gospel to the world, he wandered through the streets and byways.... All he wanted was a few men who would think as he did, love as he did, see as he did, teach as he did, and serve as he did. All he needed was to revolutionize the hearts of a few, and they would impact the world."[1]

The great thing is that you don't have to wonder where you should start being the message. The answer is simple: start right where you are. The folks you interact with every day are the very people God has chosen you to be the message to—the lonely old man who lives next-door, the stressed single mom you see at work every day, the kid you notice sitting by himself at lunch. Consider loving them your personal assignment. And it's a tough one.

Being the gospel always requires us to step out of our world and into someone else's. It will require you to leave your comfort zone and step into someone else's hardship and mess.

MOVE INTO THE NEIGHBORHOOD

Jesus Christ, God Himself, left His perfect home in heaven and entered our messy world. He became human flesh so we could understand His life message. As the paraphrase of the Bible called The Message puts it, "The Word became flesh and blood, and moved into the neighborhood" (John 1:14).

If you want to be the gospel to others, you have to move into their world.

Several years ago Chris said, "Kerry, I found a great thing for you to do with the boys! One of the biggest music festivals in the world is called Bonnaroo, and it's held in Manchester, Tennessee, every year. They have all these great bands scheduled, and you could camp out there with the boys for a few days."

The camping part didn't exactly thrill me, but I was very interested in doing something with our sons, so we loaded up our gear and headed to Tennessee.

One of the first things we did was to set up our tent with a hundred thousand of our closest friends in an enormous cornfield they'd made into a campground. I grew up on the cusp of the radical sixties and seventies and had heard about music festivals like Woodstock but had never experienced them. Being at Bonnaroo that first day seemed a little like what I imagined those classic-rock festivals to have been. And it was pretty awesome.

At first.

With our tent in place, we walked over to the registration tent, where they gave us wristbands. (I'm not sure why they used wristbands. No one ever checked them during the entire weekend.) While we were going through registration, a girl who was working there asked, "Aren't you a pastor?"

I said, "Do I look like a pastor?"

"Yeah," she replied. "You're that pastor at Woodlands Church. I've actually been to your church. And you are here at Bonnaroo?"

"I'm here with my kids," I explained. "Just here to enjoy the music."

She nodded. "That's really cool."

I was smiling proudly and feeling pretty great about myself, but not for long.

When we got to the main tent and wedged ourselves into the crowd of a hundred thousand people in ninety-five-degree heat with 100 percent humidity, it was anything but cool. I quickly discovered that the only rest rooms were Porta Johns, that there weren't very many of them, and that the ones they had were filthy.

And it was a little disconcerting when I learned they had no showers.

So that first day was a mental challenge. It was hot, and we were dripping with sweat, but I told myself that somehow it would get better.

Actually, what we experienced that day was nothing like what happened next. Imagine blazing heat, no showers, sleeping on the ground—and then torrential rain.

Before the weekend was over, we were packed in tight with people elbow to elbow, tramping through ankle-deep mud. In spite of my best intentions, I was miserable.

Now, when you're in a situation like that, you have choices. You focus on how bad it is and how much you dislike the circumstances. Or you surrender to the circumstances and deal with it.

Or you call your wife.

I think I did all three.

After griping about how miserable I was, I finally did my best to relax, and before long we started having fun.

We spent the first day and most of the night listening to great bands, then finally trudged back to our tent at three in the morning. Our tent was near the stages, and the bands were still playing, so I lay there and listened until I finally drifted off to sleep.

When I awoke the next morning before the sun came up, it was already ninety-three degrees. The sun blazed through the gap in our tent flap. I checked my phone for the time and saw it was five thirty. I'd been asleep all of two hours.

That's when I knew I was in trouble. I got out of my puddle of sweat and stepped outside to call Chris.

"Pray for me," I said when she answered the phone. "Really, really pray for me. I don't think I'm going to make it."

She said, "Well, is it fun?"

"Oh, it's great to be here with the boys," I replied, "and the music is good. But this is crazy. Chris, I don't know if I can make it."

I hoped for a little sympathy. Instead she said, "Kerry, pull it together. Remember to be all there."

That's our phrase: "be all there." Wherever you are, be all there.

But right then, being "all there" was a living nightmare.

I said, "Well, first of all, I'm pretty sure that no one here is all there. I think they come here to smoke stuff that makes them feel like they are not all there. And if I stay here much longer, I might join them."

About an hour later Chris called back. She'd found us a room at a motel down the road. Normally, they were booked solid years in advance of the festival dates, but they'd had a cancellation, and one room was available. Wow. I love my wife. We packed up and went to the motel for air conditioning and a shower.

That gave us all a second wind, and we went back to the festival and had a blast.

In all of the misery, adventure, and experience of the rock festival, I learned a lesson about life.

I realized that the times when my kids feel the most loved by me is when I move into their world. I was covered in sweat, mud, and mosquito bites, but it was worth it to engage with my sons.

I also realized that's what Jesus did for us. He moved into our world. He didn't wait for us to get cleaned up and get our act together.

And I realized this is what we're called to do—to enter into the world of others, to move into their neighborhood, no matter how messy, and to be the gospel to them.

A New Understanding

As you journey toward being the message, be prepared to encounter a host of fresh perspectives and a new understanding of the people around you. You will understand the gospel in a new way, not just as a bunch of Bible books or expository sermons, but as the life of Jesus that we carry in us to the people around us.

You'll also begin to grasp what the gospel isn't. It's not so much about what you say (though that, of course, is part of it). The gospel is in you. And you are to carry it into the world. The gospel is who we are, what we do, and how we show Jesus to the world around us.

It's time to wake up to the astounding and life-altering truth that *you* are the gospel.

The Divine Whisper

1. Read John 1:14 from The Message out loud: "The Word became flesh and blood, and moved into the neighborhood."
2. Pull an empty chair beside you to remind you that the author of the Bible is right next to you.
3. Spend five minutes in silence, listening to the Word speak to your heart. Thank Him that He moved into your mess so you could understand His message of grace.

Love the One in Front of You

1. Move into someone else's world by doing something together that this person likes to do.
2. Go to a homeless shelter, and enter the world of the homeless. Ask the leaders of the shelter what you can do to help.

Part 2

Discovering...

Your Unique Life Message

*I*f you are a believer, God is at work transforming your life. If you are not a believer, God is at work leading you to Himself. Either way, He is writing a message on your life.

And what He is writing is unique to you. What's exciting is that your message is not just one of a million identical messages He's writing. No, the message He's writing on your life is uniquely yours, based on the one-of-a-kind experiences and challenges of your life.

In the bigger picture, as we've discovered, your life message is the person of Jesus Christ. He is in you; in that sense, you are the gospel. And as you prepare to carry the gospel into the world, God is shaping you in a special way to be the message to those around you.

Understanding your uniqueness can be as simple as turning to the place in your life where you've experienced the most pain and failure. This is important because it's most likely the place where you've also received the most grace.

We're conditioned to run from pain. We're conditioned to think of pain as a bad thing, a sign that we're doing something wrong. Sometimes that's exactly what it is. Pain is the result of a fallen world and often is the outcome of sin. At other times, however, the pain in our lives is the very thing God uses to help us engage with the world. The world is hurting. Having experienced our own hurts, we can more readily identify with the hurts that exist in others. In chapter 4 we'll look at how God can take our pain and turn it into His purpose.

God also uses our failures to help us find our life message. God has a way of taking our greatest messes and turning them into our greatest message. The problem is we usually try to cover up our mistakes. We try to hide our failures and weaknesses and just show people our successes and strengths. In chapter 5 we'll see that admitting our failures is the only way for our message to break through the noise of our culture and point people to the gospel.

We won't discover the uniqueness of our life message without listening to God. And for many of us that requires shutting out the noise of the world and discovering, as we call it, "the power of quiet." Chapter 6 explores new approaches to "God time," suggests ways of listening for God's gentle whisper, and offers proven spiritual disciplines to equip us as we head into the world.

One of the most important things God uses to awaken us to our unique life message is something we call "holy disturbance." Many times it's anger that wells up over injustice, or it's pain we see in the world around us. The feeling "That's just not right!" is something God uses to push us out of our comfort zones and into living out our life message. In chapter 7 we'll dig into the question "What disturbs you and makes you angry?"

As you read the next four chapters and prepare yourself to be the gospel in your world, take time to think deeply about how God is shaping your life message for a distinct purpose. Open yourself to the tough questions about your own hurts and failures, and listen for God's gentle whisper about the specific needs in people for whom He is preparing you.

God never wastes a hurt.
He can turn our pain into
His purpose.
#BeTheMessage

4

God's Megaphone

*God whispers to us in our pleasures, speaks in
our consciences, but shouts in our pains. It is his
megaphone to rouse a deaf world.*

C. S. Lewis

*When we honestly ask ourselves which person in
our lives means the most to us, we often find that
it is those who, instead of giving advice, solutions
or cures, have chosen rather to share our pain and
touch our wounds with a warm and tender hand.*

Henri J. M. Nouwen

The most powerful message ever preached at our church was not given by
me.

It was the life message of a baby girl named Jamie Faith Douglas. She
never spoke a word, but her little life became a sacred shout that has brought
the gospel to thousands.

Reid Douglas grew up in our church. As a kid, he participated in the
children's ministry. He came to a firsthand faith in Christ while a member of

our student ministry. He went off to college and married a wonderful young lady, Rachel, who also loved the Lord. They had a baby boy named Jack and, soon after, a baby girl, whom they named Jamie Faith.

When Jamie was born, she looked perfect. She had bright blue eyes and a beautiful countenance. But a few months later Reid and Rachel realized that Jamie was not developing the way she should. After several rounds of tests, doctors diagnosed her with a rare congenital brain defect. It was considered terminal.

Reid and Rachel prayed for God's healing and strength, and the whole church gathered around them.

While Jamie was in the hospital, Reid started reading the book *More Than a Carpenter* by Josh McDowell. It was written to help people who wrestle with questions about God, to offer assurance to those who have doubts about their faith. God used that book to help Reid and Rachel through their questions and pain.

As Jamie's condition worsened, a long stream of family, friends, and church members came to the hospital to sit with Reid and Rachel. Some prayed with them. Some just sat and talked. The reaction of those visitors and the strength evident in Reid and Rachel made an impression on the hospital staff and on our members as well. Jamie's life might have been short, but it became a moment of spiritual renewal and growth for many.

The night before Jamie died, I went over to pray with them. While I was there, Reid mentioned Josh McDowell's book and said, "I've been giving copies of it to all the doctors and nurses. They come in here and look at Jamie and, in spite of her condition, think something's amazing about her. She can't say a word, and we don't know what's going on in her mind, but something about her is shouting to everybody."

Not long after Jamie Faith passed into God's loving arms, people wrestling with their own experiences of losing a loved one began coming to Reid and Rachel, mostly so they could talk with someone who could understand their pain. They found not only a sympathetic ear but also a couple who could point them toward a real and lasting healer.

Reid and Rachel now minister to hundreds of parents whose children have serious illnesses. Their pain has given them a unique message.

At Jamie Faith's funeral, our chapel was filled to overflowing with people who had been touched by her all-too-brief life. When the service ended, Reid and Rachel said to everyone, "Before you leave the funeral, Jamie Faith has one more gift for you. It's a book that will point you to the only One who can heal your hurts and bring you to heaven one day."

They gave everyone in attendance a copy of *More Than a Carpenter.*

Jamie Faith's story and the pain her parents experienced through it continue to shout the gospel even today.

Our Christmas Eve services, attended by more than forty thousand people each year, include many who make the holiday service a family tradition. Some who attend celebrate Christmas but have never really experienced the Christ of Christmas.

This past year at the Christmas Eve service, we showed a video of Jamie's story. It talked about how God brought light and hope in the darkest night of Reid and Rachel's lives. After the video I said, "If you are a skeptic, agnostic, or atheist, Jamie Faith has a gift for you. We want to give you the book *More Than a Carpenter* to help you in your spiritual journey."

Nine hundred thirty-four skeptics came to the foyer of the church to get Jamie's gift. We followed up with those who received the book and started a class specifically tailored toward them.

Jamie Faith, without saying a word, continues to shout the gospel to a hurting world. I have a feeling that many more miracles are on the way as the ripple effect of her brief life increases.

Until we get to heaven, we may never understand why God called Jamie home after only ten months. That question continues to linger without a clear answer. The pain and grief are still raw and deep for Rachel and Reid, but they also have a growing sense of peace as they see God turning their greatest pain into their greatest purpose.

SACRED SHOUT

Pain, of course, takes many forms. Sometimes the pain is the death of someone close to us, like the loss of a child, spouse, or parent. Other times pain is a physical illness or injury, something that puts us through a medical ordeal and perhaps a difficult recovery. Pain can come in the form of a circumstance that befalls us—getting passed over for a promotion, experiencing a financial setback, losing a job.

Whatever the source of pain or its degree of hurt, we need to see pain as having special properties. It may offer us opportunities in our lives.

C. S. Lewis said that pain is the megaphone God uses to break through the noise of our lives.[1] God uses our pain to get our attention. It's the "sacred shout." While on this earth we will never fully understand why bad things happen. The deeper truth is that hidden within pain, hardship, and suffering are the keys to "being the message."

Pain, by its very nature, is transformational. It never leaves us where it finds us. It changes us and moves us to a new place intellectually, emotionally, spiritually, and sometimes even physically. It's important for us to use our pain for a greater good, to be aware that this experience is equipping us in some significant, if mysterious, way to form our unique life message.

God calls us through the megaphone of pain. When pain enters our lives, instead of doubting God's purpose, we can gain insight by asking ourselves three questions:

"What does God want me to learn through this experience?"

"How is God using this experience to give me a unique message?"

"Through this experience, where is God directing me?"

LEARNING

What does God want me to learn through this experience?

When pain comes into our lives, many of us make the mistake of assuming God is punishing us. This contributes to even deeper anguish. We might wonder, *What did I do so wrong to deserve this?*

Yes, God is just, and He does punish sin. But more often than not, pain is the result of circumstances that simply happen in a fallen world. Bad things happen.

God can bring something good out of a bad experience. In these painful situations God often shows an astonishing display of grace and power. He literally takes the destructive work of the Enemy and turns it into something beautiful.

When we look to God for something beautiful and amazing, when we watch and learn, we participate in this remarkable thing that God is doing in our lives. While we are enduring the pain and the difficulty, we also are watching God work.

From that we grow and deepen, and we become better equipped to live out the gospel.

One thing you might learn from a painful experience is the strength God gives you to face it. In fact, there are many things in life that we fear, avoid, even run from. Sometimes it's a hurtful experience that brings us to that moment of truth, and we're surprised that we're actually able to face it with courage and strength. People often never really know themselves until they face a difficult circumstance for the first time. God's megaphone brings us into that moment of truth.

The experience of pain in our lives also makes us sensitive to pain in others' lives. We may then become more deeply aware of a need that we are uniquely gifted to meet.

When I (Chris) was a teenager, my mother was suddenly diagnosed with stage-four colorectal cancer. The news came as a gut punch to my whole family, and we felt inadequate and insecure as we reluctantly stepped into the world of cancer.

Tests, surgery, chemotherapy, radiation, exams, appointments, referrals, pills, transfusions, nausea, hair loss—every aspect of the journey was unfamiliar and daunting. Pain was the only constant.

As her illness progressed, we moved further into uncharted territory. Palliative care, end-of-life decisions, and, finally, funeral arrangements, which were nearly our undoing. The sheer stress of managing details and making decisions on top of our frayed nerves and raw pain was almost unbearable.

At the time I didn't know anyone who had been through a similar situation of having an immediate family member with cancer or losing a parent. And I didn't want to burden my dad and sisters with my pain because I knew they were already experiencing enough of their own. I had well-meaning friends, but they couldn't possibly understand what I was going through. If only I could have talked to one person who understood! Of course, the pain of seeing my mom so sick would have still been there, but sharing my hurt would have lifted heavy rocks from my chest.

The crucible of cancer opened my eyes to the needs of other hurting people. It made me want to notice other people's pain instead of their mistakes.

Shortly after my mom's death, I went through training to become a hospice caregiver, and our church now has an extensive Cancer Care Ministry to meet the unique needs of cancer patients and their families.

Pain gives us an education into the suffering of others and a much deeper sense of empathy. That kind of heartache for others can motivate us to action. Our understanding of someone else's hurt is now more vivid and intense, so much so that we get up and finally do something about it.

The things you learn from your experiences will be unique to you, and they contribute to your personal life message. But I can tell you that one part of that learning will very likely be this: a new experience of God's presence in your life.

When we go through difficulty and pain, we experience God's presence in a new way. He is always there, but we're not always paying attention. God's megaphone gets our attention, and in the midst of the painful circumstance, we are more deeply focused on God's presence and His comfort.

As we come alongside others who are going through circumstances similar to those we've endured, not only can we identify with their pain, but we can watch expectantly for the ways God will be present in their lives.

The most spiritually mature and Christlike people I (Chris) know are those who have experienced great pain and loss. They recognize that the pain has scarred them, and instead of trying to quickly move on from the heartache, they move deeper into God's arms.

One of these special people is Kay Warren. She and her husband, Rick, have been mentors and friends who have truly modeled for Kerry and me what it means to be the message. Approaching the one-year anniversary of the death of their precious son, Matthew, Kay wrote a powerful piece on the well-meaning but often insensitive comments she's received during the grieving process. Kay posted her piece titled "Don't Tell Grievers to 'Move On'" on her Facebook page, and it immediately went viral.

It struck such a nerve with everyone who has grieved a loss that it was read by more than three million people in just a few days. Kay wrote so profoundly about how grief is a long and messy process that deserves to be respected and not minimized. In one part of her post she wrote,

> They want the old Rick and Kay back. They secretly wonder when things will get back to normal for us—when we'll be ourselves, when the tragedy of April 5, 2013 will cease to be the grid that we pass everything across. And I have to tell you—the old Rick and Kay are gone. They're never coming back. We will never be the same again. There is a new "normal." April 5, 2013 has permanently marked us. It will remain the grid we pass everything across for an indeterminate amount of time…maybe forever.

In our culture we try to avoid pain at all costs, and we often selfishly want others who are going through pain to "get through it." The people, however, whom I've learned the most from are those who are honest about their pain and heartache and who acknowledge that the pain has fundamentally changed them.

Kay Warren never set out to be an encouragement to millions of people who have gone through grief. She just honestly shared her raw and real pain without running from it, and God continues to lift her up as a profound and powerful voice that cuts through all the lifeless pseudo-Christian clichés about pain and suffering.

A person whose life has been permanently marked by pain and yet is still standing is the loudest and clearest life message to a hurting and lost world. Pain is God's megaphone in our lives to get our attention, but it's also the pain in our lives that shouts to a hurting world that the gospel is alive and that God is real. When we cover up our pain, it not only hinders our healing, but it also muffles our message.

BECOMING

Instead of covering your pain, ask yourself, *How is God using this experience to give me a unique message?*

I think God often uses difficult circumstances to shake up our time and focus. We run the rat race, we chase after goals, we are consumed with our routines—and God puts a brief stop to all of it, raises His megaphone, and says, "Look over here. Think about this instead. Here is the unique thing I gifted you with, and here's how you can use it."

After World War II ended, Truett Cathy started a little restaurant in Georgia with his brother. It was just a little diner that never did very well. Several years after they started the business, Cathy's brother was tragically killed in a plane crash. Cathy was devastated by the loss. Not long after that, the restaurant caught fire and burned to the ground. Then Cathy was hit with a health crisis and underwent major surgery that confined him to a hospital bed for two months. As he lay in that hospital bed, he prayed and asked God to give him some new ideas and direction, for both his business and his life.

Now, Cathy loved chicken. It was his favorite food. While he was in the hospital, he came up with the idea of putting a chicken breast on a bun, of making a sandwich out of chicken.

Chick-fil-A was born.

He would later say, "My kids are so glad I was laid up in that bed for two months." Truett Cathy interpreted being laid up in bed as God telling him to stop and refocus.

I've talked with quite a few people who've experienced the loss of a job. They were laid off, or their company phased them out, or they were abruptly fired. One man told me, "You know, five years ago I lost my job, and I didn't know what I was going to do. It seemed like a terrible thing at the time, but now I see it was the very thing that God used to refocus me, point me in a new direction. Losing my job was the best thing that ever happened to me because I wouldn't have even considered what I'm doing now as a possibility."

God never wastes hurt and anguish. Remember Joseph? He was sold into slavery by his brothers, then put in prison for a crime he didn't commit. I'm sure in prison he must have asked God, "Why?" Joseph had lived an exemplary life. He had followed the rules and conducted himself with integrity, but still the trouble just kept coming. Despite that, Joseph continued to trust that God still had a plan for his life, and he believed that even in the midst of the pain, he was right in the middle of God's will.

God didn't remove the pain. Instead, He focused Joseph on his unique gift, the interpretation of dreams, and that became the pathway that led Joseph into Pharaoh's court. God used Joseph's problems to enable his gift, and his gift catapulted him to second in command over all Egypt. And in that position he was able to save his family—the people of Israel—from extinction in the great famine that followed.

At the end of it all, Joseph was able to say to his brothers, who had sold him into slavery, "You intended to harm me, but God intended it for good to accomplish what is now being done, the saving of many lives" (Genesis 50:20).

God took the work of evil and astonishingly turned it into good.

DOING

Through this experience, where is God directing me?

Sometimes the pain we experience and the things we learn while wrestling through it point us to a new ministry and life message that others need.

The apostle Paul said, "He comes alongside us when we go through hard times, and before you know it, he brings us alongside someone else who is going through hard times so that we can be there for that person just as God was there for us" (2 Corinthians 1:4, MSG).

As you study your hardship or circumstance to learn what God is telling you and lean into your pain for an indication of the unique message it might equip you to have, you should also consider what this difficult time might be pointing you to do and how it might compel you to act.

You might think that's impossible. You might already be asking yourself, *From the confines of a hospital bed or a wheelchair or a mountain of debt, how can I help someone else?*

But it's in those moments of impossibility that God does some of His best work.

Nick Vujicic is a good friend of mine. He's also one of the best communicators of the gospel I know. Nick was born with no arms or legs, and the doctors have no idea what caused such severe congenital defects.

In spite of Nick's physical issues, God has raised him up as a great voice to people around the world as he shares how he found true joy in Christ. People who are hurting find a unique connection to him as he talks about his struggles. His life message is an incredibly powerful expression of the gospel.

Nick shares his message in the United States and all over the world. In some third-world countries Nick travels to, people with physical handicaps are seen as worthless. Babies born with physical defects are sometimes left for dead in the trash heap because they are considered burdens. Nick speaks directly into this terrible problem simply by being onstage, sharing his purpose and the meaning he finds in Christ. The words he says come directly from the life he lives, and because of that, they carry divine weight.

Not only is his message a word of hope to those facing similar trouble, but many parents who have children with handicaps learn to see their children in a new light. They hear Nick's message of hope as he speaks, but more important, they see the message of hope in his life.

I once asked Nick, "If God came to you and said, 'Nick, I'll give you arms and legs right now if you want,' what would you say?"

Nick told me emphatically, "No," and went on to say, "I realize now that God has allowed me to have this handicap so that His name is glorified even more. Don't get me wrong, I used to question God all the time, and there are still many times when life gets really frustrating and I get angry. But I know God is using me to share the gospel by using my handicap to share His message of hope."

WHERE THERE'S A WALL, THERE'S A WAY

In one of the most misquoted verses in the Bible, Romans 8:28 tells us, "Moreover we know that to those who love God, who are called according to his plan, everything that happens fits into a pattern for good" (Phillips). It doesn't say that everything that comes into our lives is good. Nor does it say that everything will always work out right. Some of the things we encounter are deeply hurtful, and despite whatever good comes of it, that pain will still be there.

So I don't intend any of what I'm saying here as one of those trite everything's-going-to-work-out-right answers. The trouble we face is real and has real consequences. Bad things do happen. Tragedies befall each one of our lives. Disease occurs. Accidents happen. Terrorism is a reality in our world. People you thought were your friends will stab you in the back and wound you deeply. You'll encounter problems and troubles that knock you to your knees. You'll face obstacles that seem insurmountable and threaten to overwhelm you.

But the good news is this: God can turn your greatest barrier into the bridge that takes you to your destiny. He can take that wall you're facing and make it your greatest opportunity.

What barrier are you facing right now? Could it be that what you see as your greatest obstacle might be the bridge God wants to use to get you where you need to be? Could it be that your greatest pain is something God wants to use to propel you into your greatest purpose?

I encourage you to explore the pain you're experiencing in your life.

Sometimes pain is the ink God uses to write His message on our lives.

The Divine Whisper

1. Read 2 Corinthians 1:4 in The Message: "He comes alongside us when we go through hard times, and before you know it, he brings us alongside someone else who is going through hard times so that we can be there for that person just as God was there for us."
2. Pray and thank God for how He brings comfort and healing in your pain.
3. Ask God to show you how He wants to use your pain in your life message.
4. Spend five minutes in silence letting God heal and restore your emotions.

Love the One in Front of You

1. Look for a way in your church or community to come alongside someone who is going through a problem you've already been through.
2. Remember when you are talking to someone going through pain that God doesn't call you to have all the answers. He calls you to be the love and compassion of Christ to that person.

Don't hide your failures.
Your greatest mess is what
God uses to become your
greatest message.

#BeTheMessage

5

From Mess to Message

My grace is sufficient for you, for my power is made perfect in weakness.
2 Corinthians 12:9

If the Gospels were truly the pattern of God's activity, then defeat was only the beginning.
Corrie ten Boom

One of the things I've learned about the gospel is that everything is flipped. Jesus had a way of turning everything upside down.

For example, you expect God to use your strengths and successes—the times when you persevered, overcame, and endured without compromise—and of course He does.

More often, however, He makes use of your weaknesses and failures to accomplish His purposes. God made this point directly when He said to the apostle Paul, "My grace is sufficient for you, for my power is made perfect in weakness" (2 Corinthians 12:9).

THE MESSY LIFE GOD REDEEMS

Many times our strongest life message comes from our biggest mess. We usually try to cover up our failures and weaknesses, but it's those very failures—the ones we try to hide—that draw people to us and help them hear the gospel from us.

Brenda Spahn headed a tax consulting firm in Birmingham, Alabama. One day she drove up to her offices to find several cop cars in front. People were carrying out boxes of files and papers from her place of business.

She was being raided by the authorities.

It turned out that one of her clients was under investigation for a number of improprieties, among them tax fraud. Brenda and her employees did not knowingly do anything illegal, but they were implicated, and some irregularities were found, putting them at risk legally.

Brenda faced the possibility of doing time in prison. Nearby was Tutwiler Prison, one of the worst female prisons in the country. Brenda would sometimes drive by the prison and become increasingly fearful that she would wind up there.

Brenda's life had become a terrible mess.

The legal process was laborious, but through a series of circumstances, the charges were eventually dropped. Brenda and her company were not indicted for any crime, although she was acutely aware that the legal process could have ended badly.

She was also waking up to the fact that God had miraculously intervened.

Out of that mess Brenda discovered her life message. She founded a unique kind of halfway house to serve the needs of female ex-cons coming out of Tutwiler. She knew that the usual discharge process—to send an ex-con back to her hometown, usually the place where she had gotten into trouble and into crime in the first place—made no sense. Brenda wanted to create a place where women could discover a new life, learn skills that could garner them a job, and develop maturity in their relationships.

She referred to her project as a "whole-way house" because she had learned that most halfway houses didn't work. Brenda realized that to truly show the whole way to freedom and transformation, a life of faith was essential. That whole-way house became the Lovelady Center, and it has become a model for corrections around the country.

When Brenda found herself in a mess, God invaded her world. She continues to learn about the power of God to transform messes as she works with hurting women. From the ashes of her mess, she has discovered her message.

We've had several business executives in our church speak to our students and young professionals about what they've learned through their work experience. Everyone enjoys hearing the inside stories of their successes and accomplishments, but when they share about their greatest failures, including heartbreaking accounts of bankruptcy, business collapses, and gut-wrenching losses, you can hear a pin drop.

You might think that hearing about failures would scare away those seeking a similarly brilliant career, but exactly the opposite is true. Young businessmen and businesswomen are encouraged when they hear that an obviously successful person—the executive right there in front of them— experienced failure, learned from it, and rose above it.

The pain they share gives authenticity to their message.

The people I know whose lives are the most inspiring are those who have gone through great trials and have learned to live in the tension between strength and weakness. We don't like to admit our weaknesses, but revealing them is what allows God's strength to show through.

FALLING DOWN ON THE JOB

Several years ago I was speaking in the Sunday morning service when for no obvious reason I became dizzy. The room began to spin, and my hands became sweaty. My heart started racing, and I said, "Folks, I'm not feeling well. I need to sit down."

As I made my way to a chair, I noticed people in the congregation were smiling. We are known for doing creative, unexpected things, so a number of people laughed. Some whispered to those around them, "Oh this is going to be good. This skit is going to be amazing." One told the visitor next to him, "We do this stuff all the time. He's just kidding. It's going to be awesome. You're going to love it."

But it wasn't a skit, and I wasn't kidding, and soon the crowd got quiet.

Our worship team stepped in and led the congregation in a couple of songs to help fill in the time while I closed my eyes and tried to figure out what to do next. After a few minutes I was feeling better, so I pushed on through and finished the service.

By the afternoon I was feeling fine. I'd had the flu a few weeks earlier and attributed the dizziness to that, the residual effects of a virus.

I didn't think much more about the incident until the following week when I got up to preach again. Suddenly I experienced the same symptoms, so much so that I was worried about what would happen if I fainted right there on the stage. Again I made it through the services that day without a major incident, but the following week it happened a third time.

Later that week a trip to the doctor and a round of tests revealed no physical cause. It was a mystery illness.

Over the next few weeks, the sensation dissipated during the worship services, but at night I would awaken in bed, sweaty and dizzy, my heart racing. Another trip to the doctor still revealed no physical cause.

One day a friend said, "Sounds to me as if you're having panic attacks. That's what this looks like. A classic panic attack."

I said, "No, no, no. It's not a mental thing. It's physical, not psychological." To be honest, I was afraid that my emotional and psychological issues were spiritual deficiencies in disguise. Maybe I just wasn't spiritual enough. Right away guilt and condemnation rushed in.

After wrestling with that possibility for a few days, I eventually gave in and called a friend who is a Christian counselor and physician. Through him, I learned about anxiety attacks and my own psychological history. God began an amazing healing process in my soul, spirit, and emotions.

When I shared my story with our congregation, everyone became quiet. People were deeply engaged with my story and my problem. What I feared would be perceived as a weakness was actually an opportunity for people to come alongside me and offer support.

Perhaps they could see something of their own situations in mine. I don't know. But I do know that, difficult as that was for me, it revealed a pointedly biblical truth. Paul elaborated on it when he said, "Therefore I will boast all the more gladly about my weaknesses, so that Christ's power may rest on me. That is why, for Christ's sake, I delight in weaknesses, in insults, in hardships, in persecutions, in difficulties. For when I am weak, then I am strong" (2 Corinthians 12:9–10).

God taught my sons and me (Kerry) about mess and grace through a humorous but memorable experience. One day when our children were much younger, I decided to take our sons to a Houston Astros baseball game. As we were preparing to leave the house for the drive to the stadium, our youngest son, Steven, picked up his baseball glove and said, "Dad, I want to take my glove to the game."

I guess every kid dreams of catching a ball at the baseball park, and that's what I assumed Steven wanted. Dreams are important at any age, and I didn't want to discourage his by telling him the chances were slim a ball would be hit as high as we would be sitting. Our seats were up in the nosebleed section, far above where balls landed.

Chris heard him talking, and before I could respond, she said, "Steven, don't take your glove. You'll have to keep up with it all day. You don't want to lose it before your big game tomorrow."

"Honey," I chimed in, "don't worry. I've got it covered."

"Okay," she replied, pointing at me, "but it's your responsibility. Be sure to get back home with it. That's the glove he uses in Little League."

I said, "No problem."

When we arrived at the ballpark, the first thing we did was visit the rest room. Steven had his glove resting on top of his head. Kids do that all the time. I did it with my glove when I was a boy, so I didn't think much of it.

Then I heard Steven yell.

Two kids are in a public rest room. And one of them is screaming. You can imagine the images that ran through my mind of all the things that might be wrong. I darted over to the stall where Steven was standing and looked over his shoulder to see what was wrong.

That's when I saw the baseball glove lying in the toilet.

Being a dad has many special privileges. We get to accompany our children on many adventures, like sleeping in a tent at music festivals, hiking through the woods when you'd rather be home soaking up the air conditioning, and a hundred other things. We also get to perform those duties no one else wants to do, like fishing a baseball glove out of a public toilet.

With as little fanfare as possible, I reached down and lifted the glove out of the water. It was soaking wet.

Our oldest son, Ryan, said, "Throw it away, Dad. Just throw it away. That's awful!"

Under other circumstances I might have done just that, but the dream of a young boy was hanging in the balance, and my wife's final words were ringing in my ears. As I backed away from the toilet, holding the glove with the tips of my fingers, I thought, *This is important to Steven and to me too. He needs his dream, and I need to bring this glove home.*

So I dropped the glove into the sink and turned on the faucet. I let the water run over it for several minutes and then scrubbed it down with soap. I cleaned it as best I could, and then I handed it to Steven. It was still dripping water.

A few minutes later we reached our seats, and I settled in to watch the Astros warm up. After a while I looked around, and Steven was gone. I leaned over to Ryan and asked, "Where's Steven?"

He nodded toward the far side of the field. "Over by the dugout trying to get some autographs."

I looked up in time to see Steven, his arm stretched over the railing, handing his soaking-wet glove to the Astros' head coach. While I watched, the coach took the glove, looked at it a moment—I'm sure wondering why it was so wet—then signed his name and handed it back. That coach had no idea where the glove had been before he took it from Steven, but in a matter of minutes it had gone from the toilet at Minute Maid Park to the hands of the Astros' head coach.

In many ways the story of that glove is the story of us all.

Regardless of who we are or how we live, we've all made a mess of our lives. But God stepped into that messy situation, lifted us out of the stench, and said with a smile, "You're Mine." He cleans us up and begins taking us to places we could never have imagined. He loves us just as we are, but He doesn't leave us that way.

This is the story of what grace can do with the mess of our lives.

THE BEAUTY OF BROKENNESS

The world tends to have a particular view of the church. It sees it as a collection of people trying really hard to be perfect, people who get a pep talk from the preacher on Sundays to help keep them perfect through the week.

I think this is why the world looks down on church people. It resents those who don't acknowledge that pain and troubles are part of being human. There are a lot of churchgoers who think the same thing—that church is about trying to follow rules and be as perfect as possible. And some churches contribute to the perception problem by projecting that image to the world.

Our oldest sons, Ryan and Josh, wrote a book called *Firsthand,* which tells of their journey to move away from a secondhand faith they inherited from us, their parents. Their book has had a huge impact on the lives of thousands of young men and women who have been turned off by what they've seen from Christians and churches who put forward an image of perfection. I think the reason God has used the book in such a powerful way is that Ryan and Josh shared honestly about their personal struggles. In the chapter "Sick of Secrets," Josh wrote,

> We all know people who put Bible verses or prayers on their Facebook
> statuses or tweets. I am not saying that is wrong or that they are being
> dishonest or anything like that. On the contrary, it can be very
> encouraging. But when do you ever see a tweet that says, "Where are
> You, God? I need You. Why have You left me?" When did you see a
> tweet that said, "I feel like a total failure, and it's killing me" or "Why
> can't I tell you who I really am?"
>
> We are so ready to let the world know when God is doing great

things. Yet when things take a turn for the worse, we keep it hidden. What are we so afraid of?[1]

When we as Christians project this kind of perfect image *to* the world, we set ourselves up for being judged *by* the world. The world feels inadequate around "perfect" Christians, and that feeling compels many to applaud when Christians fail. When a Christian slips up, especially a prominent public figure, the world quickly judges that person and says, "See, I told you so," and then launches the *h* word: *hypocrisy.*

But I have a surprise for you: Church is not about good people. It's about broken people.

Church is a community of people who have come face to face with their brokenness.

Brokenness is an idea the world doesn't know what to do with. Brokenness says that at the core we are fractured. Brokenness says that we cannot save ourselves. Brokenness says that no self-help program, no amount of counseling, no best-selling book can rescue us from what plagues us physically and spiritually.

The world, which likes to think of Self as a powerful, beautiful thing, can't quite accept that there's a rock bottom in life that even Self can't rescue Self from.

I don't know where or when I first encountered the phrase "coming to the end of ourselves," but that's precisely what our brokenness is about. That phrase says there's a place deep down, a rock bottom, at which there is no more Self.

I love this Bible verse from The Message: "You're blessed when you're at the end of your rope. With less of you there is more of God" (Matthew 5:3). When we're at the end of our rope, when we hit rock bottom, that's when God finally has us where He wants us and can do something miraculous.

And when He does, we experience a foundational truth of life.

This is where the most transformational life messages begin.

It's the message of the gospel in its purest form: Brokenness + Redemption = Transformation.

TRANSFORMATION

We seem to forget that the great heroes of the Bible went through this process that took them from brokenness and failure to transformation and triumph.

Jacob was a cheater.

Peter denied Christ.

David committed adultery.

Noah got drunk.

Jonah ran from God.

Gideon was insecure.

Miriam was a gossip.

Martha was a worrier.

Thomas was a doubter.

Zacchaeus was a cheater.

Elijah was depressed.

Moses stuttered.

Abraham was old.

Lazarus was dead.

I could go on and on listing heroes of the faith and their failures, problems, and weaknesses. The good news is that God loves to turn our brokenness into blessedness. God loves to take our mess and transform it and us into His miracle.

Perhaps the greatest story of life transformation is in the Bible: the conversion of the apostle Paul. Originally named Saul, he was a Jew, a Pharisee who was persecuting Christians. On the road to Damascus to capture Christian disciples and take them as prisoners back to Jerusalem, Saul was brought to his knees by a great light. He heard a voice and called out, "Who are you?"

"'I am Jesus,' the Lord answered. 'I am the one you are so cruel to. Now get up and go into the city, where you will be told what to do'" (Acts 9:5–6, CEV).

Saul obeyed. In a matter of a few days, the unbelieving Saul was rescued out of his life of persecuting Christians, encountered the living Christ, and received his special orders for the mission of his life message: to preach the gospel to the known world.

Writer and theologian N. T. Wright said, "Our task, as image-bearing, God-loving, Christ-shaped, Spirit-filled Christians, following Christ and shaping our world, is to announce redemption to the world that has discovered its fallenness, to announce healing to the world that has discovered its brokenness, to proclaim love and trust to the world that knows only exploitation, fear and suspicion."[2]

TRUE WORTH

To understand the concept of our true value, I always go back to an experience I had with my son Josh. He is a musician who lives in Nashville. Once when I was visiting him there, he took me to a vintage guitar store. We browsed for a while and came to an electric guitar from the sixties. It was scratched up, and the finish was worn in several spots. It didn't look very impressive to me.

Josh took it down for a closer look. I was shocked at the price. I said, "How could it be worth that much?" But then he plugged it in and strummed his finger across the strings. Even I, who can't play guitar, heard the rich, beautiful sound it made. Josh, who knows guitars, had recognized its value right away. Its age and scratches didn't distract him from its true worth.

We all have marks and scars from the mistakes we've made as we've gone through life. Yet God sees past them and knows our worth. He knows how they can become a life message of great value to others who are going through similar challenges.

Whatever failures might lie at the core of your life experience, identify them and embrace them. Don't meditate on the experience that produced the pain, but don't deny it either. It very well may be the arena where God can use you the most.

I first met Vicki Dimmit at the soccer field where we were watching our sons play. She and her husband were there with their children, and we struck up a conversation. She didn't tell me she'd been struggling for years with alcoholism, and I didn't tell her we had just planted a new church. We just talked, and in the course of that conversation I invited her to church.

The next Sunday she took me up on the invitation. She was surprised to find out I was the pastor.

"I wanted to run in the opposite direction," she said. "I'd been sober for eight months, but I had lived with thirty-five years of unforgiveness." Her husband insisted that they stay, and she was glad they did. "The message I heard that day sounded as if it was made just for me." The sermon focused on a passage from Paul's first letter to Timothy, verses that have guided Vicki ever since.

Vicki was helped along the way by an Alcoholics Anonymous group and sponsor. Later she went to training on how to lead a recovery ministry. She started our church's Restoration and Recovery Ministry with five people who were drawn to her life story. Since then, more than a thousand people have come through our church's Restoration Ministry and learned what Vicki discovered—that God can take our great mess and turn it into our life message.

Failure gets your attention and shows you the point of grace in your life. Responsibility motivates you to act. You feel a conviction to show others the way too.

I'm reminded of what the apostle Paul wrote to Timothy: "Christ Jesus came into the world to save sinners—of whom I am the worst. But for that very reason I was shown mercy so that in me, the worst of sinners, Christ Jesus might display his immense patience as an example for those who would believe in him and receive eternal life" (1 Timothy 1:15–16).

God began a work in Vicki one day and over the next several months led her from a life dominated by guilt and shame to a life of hope. "I learned that God can't change my past, or what I did, or what happened to me," she says, "but He could set me free from it."

WEAKNESS TO STRENGTH

When we feel weak and inadequate, we are more likely to turn to Christ's strength. Maybe you're feeling powerless right now. If so, that's actually a good place to be. Until we recognize our powerlessness, we'll never turn to the all-powerful God we serve.

Early in his life Joshua, Moses's successor as leader of Israel, met a challenge that dramatized his powerlessness in vivid detail. Moses was dead, but Joshua had no time to mourn the passing of his mentor and friend. The people were poised to enter the Promised Land, and it was his responsibility to lead them into it.

I'm sure he felt tremendous pressure to fill Moses's shoes, but stepping into a leadership role wasn't his biggest challenge. In order to reach their destination, they had to cross the Jordan River, but the river was at flood stage, and there were no bridges across it.

Three times God told Joshua to "be strong and courageous" (Joshua 1:6, 7, 9). Why do you think God told him three times? It wasn't because Joshua was hard of hearing but because he was feeling weak and afraid.

That encourages me so much. Many times I feel inadequate and terrified too. The great news is that God uses our weakness and fear to get our attention, to turn us toward His strength and courage.

This is what He did with Joshua. That process begins with strong and courageous thinking. God told Joshua not to focus on what he *couldn't* do but to focus on what God *could* do. Those words were an invitation for Joshua to adopt a different way of thinking, one that reflected God's unlimited perspective rather than Joshua's own limited viewpoint.

Changing our way of thinking will make all the difference.

In the early 1950s, doctors and scientists were of the opinion that no human could run the mile in less than four minutes. It was, so they said, physiologically and biologically impossible for a human being to run that fast. They argued that the human bone structure was wrong for it, that the human lung capacity was inadequate for it, and that the human heart was too weak to endure it.

But twenty-five-year-old Roger Bannister wasn't listening. He was busy training. On May 6, 1954, he ran the mile with a time of 3:59.4, accomplishing something everyone thought was impossible.

Now, the interesting thing is this: Just forty-seven days later, another runner ran the mile in less than four minutes. By 1957, just three years later, sixteen runners had broken the four-minute mark. What happened? Runners didn't suddenly become physically stronger in that short time. They became mentally stronger. Bannister's accomplishment and the knowledge that a four-minute mile was attainable changed the way they thought. He proved that supposed physical limitations didn't impose limits on human speed—at least not on a four-minute mile—and pointed to the fact that the only real barrier runners faced was a mental barrier.

The same is true in our lives. The greatest barriers you and I face in life more often than not come from our small way of thinking. Philippians 4:13 says, "I can do all things through Christ who strengthens me" (NKJV). Paul focused not on what he couldn't do but on what God could do through him. If you're a follower of Christ, you have the very power of Christ living in you. The same power that raised Christ from the dead is alive in you to give you the power you need in life.

God is not only with you; He lives inside you, and through His Spirit you can do far more than you ever dreamed. In his second letter to Timothy, Paul told us, "God has not given us a spirit of fear and timidity, but of power, love, and self-discipline" (1:7, NLT).

Perhaps you don't feel powerful, loving, and self-disciplined. In fact, you might feel very inadequate, unloving, and undisciplined. But don't focus on your feelings. Focus on the truth that Christ lives inside you. His power, His love, and His discipline are available to you. Christ wants to be your strength, wisdom, power, and love as He lives through you.

In fact, you don't even have to pray, "God, give me discipline." Just say, "God, thank You for Your discipline in me. Be my discipline today."

You don't have to pray, "God, give me more love." Just say, "God, love through me because You're in me."

You don't have to say, "God, I need You to give me power and strength." Just say, "God, let Your power and strength live through me as I face this obstacle."

Faith or Fear

There are two ways to live life. Either you live by fear, or you live by faith. We get to choose how we live, but our choices are limited to those two options. You can't live by faith if you are living by fear, and you can't live by fear if you are living by faith.

In the scripture we mentioned earlier, God told Joshua to lead the people across the Jordan River, but the river was at flood stage and humanly impossible to cross. And even though he heard from God, Joshua's physical circumstances didn't change. The river was just as high after God spoke as it was before.

Joshua had a choice. Believe God and live by faith, or ignore God and live by fear. Joshua chose faith. He probably still felt weak and afraid, but he didn't let his feelings keep him from doing what God had told him to do. And what had God told him? "Be strong and courageous." He didn't say, "Feel strong and courageous." God said, "Be."

Courage isn't what you do when you feel confident and adequate. Courage is what you do when you feel least confident and least adequate. When we act with courage, regardless of our feelings of weakness, God fills us with His strength.

Although faced with insurmountable odds and a humanly impossible situation, Joshua pointed the people toward the river and led them in that direction. As they walked, the priests led the procession. When the priests' feet touched the water, the river parted, and the people crossed on dry ground (see Joshua 3:14–16).

Sometimes God calls us to take a step of faith in spite of our weakness and fear *before* He opens up the path ahead.

Step into the river, and watch as God works a miracle. Admit your weaknesses, fears, and insecurities to God, and take that first step into His strength and courage.

You can live by fear or by faith. The choice is yours.

YOUR MIGHTY MESSAGE OF WEAKNESS

I have found the movie *Apollo 13* to be a story that illustrates so many important things in life. It depicts enormous courage and power in the face of failure and weakness. One scene in particular speaks volumes.

The *Apollo 13* spacecraft has just gone through an explosion, rendering it helpless. As it floats through space, mission control tries everything to figure out how to bring the astronauts back to earth alive. Gene Kranz, lead flight director, is mobilizing every person he can to conjure up solutions for saving the crew.

In the midst of great despair, the NASA director says, "This could be the worst disaster NASA's ever experienced."

And Kranz replies, "With all due respect, sir, I believe this is going to be our finest hour."

Our message of weakness is very possibly, in the hands of God, our finest hour. We can live ashamed of it, we can try to hide it, and we can feel overwhelmed by it.

But if we admit our failure and are willing to be used, God can take it and transform it into our life message.

He can take shame and turn it into triumph.

And that, my friend, is the gospel.

The Divine Whisper

1. Write down some of your failures and weaknesses. This will be between you and God. Be totally honest with yourself before Him.
2. Ask God to put His strength in your weakness and to take the fear and guilt out of your failures. Give them over to God to use however He wants.
3. Read aloud 2 Corinthians 12:9: "My grace is sufficient for you, for my power is made perfect in weakness."
4. Spend five minutes in silence listening for God's gentle whisper as you thank Him for turning your mess into your message.

Love the One in Front of You

1. Encourage someone today who has experienced a recent failure.
2. Do you know people who have recently made a mess of their lives? Pray for God to turn their messes into life messages.
3. Share one of your greatest mistakes with someone this week. Ask the person to pray that God will show you how to begin using it to shape your life message.

If you want your message
to be clearly heard,
then you must clearly listen.
#BeTheMessage

6

The Power of Quiet

While you were doing all these things, declares the
LORD, *I spoke to you again and again, but you did*
not listen.

Jeremiah 7:13

Somewhere we know that without silence words
lose their meaning, that without listening speak-
ing no longer heals, that without distance closeness
cannot cure.

Henri J. M. Nouwen

I'm hoping you're beginning to form a picture of your unique life message.

The picture is outlined at first in blood—the blood of your personal pain, hurt, and anguish. Then it gets filled in with the colors of your problems, mistakes, sins, and failures. It's tinted with your personality, passions, and gifts. God paints your message on a canvas, puts it into a frame, and mounts it on the wall of life.

God stands next to the portrait of your life message and proclaims, "Behold My latest masterpiece!"

And miracle of miracles, it's beautiful. It looks like you. Totally you. Uniquely you. It's your unique life image based on your one-of-a-kind journey that can lead you to make a God-sized difference in the world.

Maybe your head is spinning with possibilities. I hope so. Maybe you're now seeing a purpose you can fulfill and ways you can help others. I encourage you to follow those ideas. Maybe you already have a plan, some next steps, an outline, a blueprint for the next stage of your life. All good.

But God is saying to you, "And now, I want you to…"

And you, unfortunately, might not be listening. You might not listen to what God is telling you next. We rarely do. We charge ahead. We talk; we schedule; we talk; we plan; we talk.

In the pursuit of living our life message, this is a fatal mistake. It's good to be excited about discovering uniqueness born out of the mess of our lives, but there's a piece of the puzzle that's missing.

And that's God Himself.

Before you begin to live out your life message and embark on the exciting mission of making a difference in the world, you have to listen to Him. His whisper.

So God is telling you, "Stop. Close your mouth. Be quiet. Listen."

This is something we've been learning in a new way, specifically in the context of discovering our life message and mission. If we really want to know what we are to do in the world, if we want to pursue those things that will truly be helpful and transforming, we need to obey Him completely. We have to listen to His whisper.

We can't simply charge ahead with our newfound life message and create our own agenda. As pastor and author Mark Batterson says in *All In*, "When we take matters into our own hands, we take God out of the equation."

We need God to be in the equation. He must be the writer of our life message in the world if we are to make a difference. Otherwise we will fail before we even begin. So how do we stop, close our mouths, stay quiet, and listen?

Well, relax, I'm not talking about "quiet time." Not as you may think of it.

I have always had a quiet time, a daily period of devotions and prayer. Nothing wrong with that. I continue to embrace this practice, and it's an important part of my spiritual life.

But quiet time often isn't really quiet. Prayer during that time can be more about talking *at* God than listening *to* Him. And even when we aren't speaking aloud, our minds are filled with voices—our own and others'—that distract us. Quiet time is usually squeezed into an early morning window, rushed by our schedule, done hastily and without our full attention or focus. It can become just a box we check off in our Christian life. It's shockingly easy to have a quiet time yet never really listen to God.

Is that true for you too?

When my daughter Megan was a senior in high school, she faced several major life decisions as she prepared to go to college. One day she posed a question that's been put to me dozens of times by people in our church. Megan asked, "How do you know what God is telling you to do? I mean, when you're faced with two options that seem a lot the same, how do you know which choice God wants you to make?"

She went on to say something I think you and I both have said and wanted at one time or another: "I wish God would give me a big sign or speak in an audible voice and just say, 'Do this' or 'Do that.'"

Well, God is often telling us precisely that, but too often we aren't quiet or still enough to hear Him.

Andrew Murray, pastor and prolific devotional author who lived in the early 1900s, wrote, "As long as in our worship of God we are chiefly occupied with our own thoughts and exercises, we shall not meet Him who is a Spirit, the unseen One. But to the man who withdraws himself from all that is of the world and man, and prepares to wait upon God alone, the Father will reveal Himself."[1]

What we've been discovering is that there are deeper levels of spending time with God. There are spiritual disciplines and practices designed to take us out of our busy lives and into a period of silence, one that isn't filled with anything but God Himself. And it's in this special time that God reveals Himself in a special way. It's here we find our marching orders for being the message and taking the gospel to our world.

Several of these spiritual practices might be helpful to you. They aren't magical or mystical. They're simply ways of getting you away from the busyness of life and into a place, both physical and spiritual, where you have intimate time with God so He can whisper to you about His plans for your life.

These are preparations for your journey ahead, a kind of boot camp or basic training for His mission. I like the way author Richard Foster put it: "And so I urge you to still every motion that is not rooted in the Kingdom. Become quiet, hushed, motionless until you are finally centered. Strip away all excess baggage and nonessential trappings until you have come into the stark reality of the Kingdom of God. Let go of all distractions until you are driven into the Core. Allow God to reshuffle your priorities and eliminate unnecessary froth."[2]

This deeper place of communion with God is where you get your special orders from Him. The journey ahead requires your unique set of hurts, pains, mistakes, failures, skills, and personality traits. In tandem with your unique life message, God has a unique mission for you.

But before you go anywhere or do anything, you have to "Stop. Close your mouth. Be quiet. Listen."

Only then can you experience the power of quiet.

Only then will you hear His divine whisper.

SILENT RETREAT

One of the spiritual practices we recommend is a silent retreat.

Often scheduled by a church or ministry, a silent retreat may be done by yourself, with a friend, or even with a small group, but the purpose is to spend time in silence to focus on God. It usually lasts a full day (from about eight o'clock in the morning to four in the afternoon) in a location that is peaceful and somewhat secluded. The goals and purposes of the retreat are defined at the start, and there may be times of individual or group worship throughout the day.

Many people are a bit fearful of spending a full day in silence and solitude. At a silent retreat, cell phones and other technology are not allowed except for emergencies. I know, that's hard to do. The fact that it's so hard points to our dependence on technology for connectedness and distraction. It also speaks to the problems that we face in our morning quiet times— when we attempt to listen to God with our Bibles in one hand and our cell phones in the other.

But that's kind of the point.

And if you commit to a day of silence, the time can be extremely re-warding.

Kent, a friend of mine, talks about his experience at a silent retreat: "I was a little apprehensive when I went the first time. I really didn't think I could go for a whole day of complete solitude. It sounded like it would be boring to me. To the contrary, it was extraordinary, and I found that I was in communion with God in a way I've never experienced before."

A silent retreat encourages Bible reading, and you can bring a book of spiritual devotions or a Bible study. And it's a time of prayer but in a different way than usual. Kent says, "Since there was so much time—a full day— prayer became less urgent and rushed. And at some point it stopped being so much about me talking and more about me listening."

We often miss God's voice because our lives are so noisy. Hearing His whisper requires diminishing the racket that screams through our daily lives, and creating a space and time when we push back against the confusion and find sacred silence.

For Kent that time of sacred silence allowed him to open his ears to listen for God's leading. "I would say it changed my life—in a quiet way. God's voice to me that day was that He embraced me personally, that I was not just one of many billions of people to Him, but I was *Kent,* unique in my stuff, and very special to Him. And the message that came out that day was huge— He wants to be with me."

LECTIO DIVINA

There is an ancient practice called *lectio divina,* which means "sacred or divine reading." This is a time-honored spiritual discipline, developed by Benedictine monks, of reading specified portions of Scripture and meditating on them in a particular way.

The lectio divina has recently become a special practice in our lives. Now, I know some people might be leery of meditation because of its prevalence in Eastern mysticism and the new-age movement. But this is different. I'm not suggesting you chant a phrase to put yourself in a trance. I'm talking about biblical meditation, which has been practiced by Christian believers for hundreds of years.

Richard Foster explains, "Whenever the Christian idea of meditation is taken seriously, there are those who assume it is synonymous with the concept of meditation centered in Eastern religions. In reality, the two ideas stand worlds apart. Eastern meditation is an attempt to empty the mind; Christian meditation is an attempt to fill the mind. The two ideas are quite different."[3]

Lectio divina is really about engaging with the Bible in a new way through reading, meditating, praying, and contemplating. A passage of Scripture is selected and read four times, using a different method for each reading. By doing this the words reveal a far deeper meaning.

You can do this on your own. For greatest effectiveness choose a time and place where you can sit quietly without being interrupted.

First, choose a passage or chapter in the Bible. Reading it aloud is fine but not necessary. Read the passage several times, perhaps one time normally but the next time slowly. The idea is to encounter what might be a familiar Bible passage in a fresh way, so any reading technique that helps shake up that familiarity is probably good.

Second, meditate on the Scripture passage, rolling the words around in your mind without assigning meaning or importance to them. This exercise is specifically designed to allow the Holy Spirit to bring to mind what He wants to specifically highlight or reveal to you. This is not a time to analyze the meaning by dissecting words and phrases. Rather, this is a process of *experiencing* Scripture. It may take a while to get used to this.

After reading and meditating, the third step is to pray the scripture. In this sense, prayer is an audible conversation with God. Speak. Choose a place to begin, any place that relates to the scripture you read, and simply start talking to Him using the words you read. It's amazing what can come from this—a new sense of God's Word to us as we repeat it to Him.

The fourth step is contemplation. Here you read the passage one more time to yourself, attentive to the meaning of the passage, to what God might be telling you, and to how the passage specifically applies to you, your life, and your life message. This is where you move from what you've seen and heard to explore what the scripture means for you in your particular context.

The lectio divina, though an ancient practice, is a fresh way of listening to God speak to us through His Word. It's nothing more than a practice of reading the Bible. It's nothing less than experiencing God's Word in a more profound, meaningful way.

THE PRACTICE OF THE PRESENCE OF GOD

One of the most useful books I've read on the power of silence and the contemplative life is entitled *The Practice of the Presence of God*. The book recounts conversations and correspondence with Nicholas Herman of Lorraine, a man who entered a Carmelite monastery as a lay member in the sixteen hundreds. Known to most of the world simply as Brother Lawrence, he was assigned menial daily tasks too disgusting for regular members of the order. Rather than complain, he gave himself over to God in those tasks and developed what he referred to as the "practice of the presence of God," the attitude of sensing God's presence with him regardless of the circumstances in which his daily life might place him.

Brother Lawrence described this practice in several ways, but in one conversation he said that for him "the set times of prayer were not different from other times; that he retired to pray, according to the directions of his superior, but that he did not want such retirement, nor ask for it, because his greatest business did not divert him from God."[4]

God is with us always. But all too rarely in our daily lives are we really aware of His presence. Brother Lawrence discovered that he could make himself aware that God was with him at any and all times, no matter what he was doing. Whether washing dishes in the kitchen or traveling to the countryside to purchase wine for the monastic community, he always sensed God's presence with him. In that way, Brother Lawrence's life became a continual conversation with God. Times in his daily schedule that were devoted to prayer and times devoted to work were one and the same.

That lesson applies to us as well. We can listen to God while standing at the kitchen sink, mowing the lawn, or doing any of the other routine tasks of the day.

Listening to God's whisper is more a way of life than it is a scheduled event.

You can practice God's presence in a number of different ways. You can spend fifteen minutes reading Scripture and listening as God speaks to your heart. On a more practical level, you can pause for ten seconds before too quickly answering a friend's question and listen, really listen, for God to give you ears to hear what your friend is really saying and wisdom to respond. That way, you'll actually have a response to give your friend that helps rather than filling the moment with meaningless words.

You can listen for the divine whisper as you sit with your spouse, listening—really listening—to what he or she is saying, or not saying. And you can listen for God's whisper when you are in a meeting and you refrain from showing everyone how much you know so you can hear what God has to say.

In short, practicing the presence of God is an intentional act in any situation to consciously focus on God's presence in that place at that moment.

SACRED SILENCE

All these spiritual practices (and others) are simply practical methods to help you make time alone with God and create an opportunity for you to hear His divine whisper. They're all designed to bring you to a place of sacred silence.

Understand that these methods are not sacred in themselves. They're not the goal but a means to the goal. However you accomplish listening to God's divine whisper, whether through these spiritual practices or others, the goal is for you to close out the noisy distractions of the world and pay attention to what God is telling you.

And He *will* tell you.

The answer to my daughter's question "How do you know what God wants you to do?" is relatively simple.

You listen.

How you listen is not really the issue, although we tend to make that too complicated. The point is that much of the time we *don't* listen, or our lives are so loud that there's no way we can hear God's whisper over the din and blare.

There's also something else going on here. When we refine our listening skills to hear God's divine whisper, we become attuned to the needs of others around us. Sacred silence is not about taking a vow of silence where you never speak. It's about a way of life that puts you in a position to become the message to the people around you.

Years ago when our son Ryan was only three or four years old, I often took him to the neighborhood park near our house. One afternoon Ryan met another little boy whose name was Loren. They played on the swings and slides as I watched from a nearby park bench. They had a good time together, and I didn't think much of it.

After a while, however, we needed to return home. So I called my son, and we got ready to leave. As we did, I noticed a car parked at the curb. Loren started toward it, and I became concerned. He was a young kid. I saw no adults at the park, which meant he was there alone. And here he was, headed toward a car. All those stories about kids and strangers flashed through my mind. So I turned to him and said, "Loren, where do you live?"

"Right here," he said, pointing to the car. "That is where I live."

His home was the car. In an instant I knew God was prompting me to do something about that. The thought of it entered my mind, and I felt the truth of it in my soul, my heart, my spirit. But in my haste, I just said, "Oh, okay," and led our son back toward the house. But the farther we walked from the park, the more dreadful I felt. I had the sense that I was walking away from something I really needed to do.

I walked back to the park and noticed the car was still there by the curb. I leaned down to the window and saw Loren's parents there. I introduced myself, then told them who I was and where our church was located. "And," I said, "I'll see what our church can do to help you. I think we can help you get back on your feet." I knew it was the right thing to do—it was what God wanted me to do—but it launched us on a long road, a road that carried its share of challenges.

Life change is messy, and it's usually the messiness that leads some churches to become a "holy huddle" rather than a caring community that reaches out. Everything about our involvement with Loren's parents was messy, but we saw God's miracles in the mess. They came to our church the next day, and after receiving food from our food pantry and hearing the gospel, they both prayed to receive Christ into their lives.

The first thing they needed was to get out of that car. So we put them in a motel room. Later that day I went to pray with them and learned they were not married. They wanted to be. They just weren't. So we found a family to take in Loren and his mom while his dad stayed at the motel and we sorted things out.

In order to address their situation, they needed a marriage license, but they had lost their birth certificates. Over the next few weeks we worked our way through those details, and they obtained the license.

We conducted a wedding ceremony for them, and the best man showed up drunk.

Not long after that, we learned the husband had a drug problem. After a stint in a rehab program, he needed a job, which we helped him find. It seemed as if their troubles would never end, but eventually we got them situated in an apartment and living on their own. Like all of our journeys, theirs was three steps forward and two steps back.

Thankfully, God can work miracles in our messes.

From the moment I learned that Loren lived in a car, I knew that God was speaking to me. I knew it in my mind, my heart, my soul, my spirit. And I knew that helping them would not be easy. That was part of the reason for my reluctance in going back to their car that day. It took me a while to align my actions with what God was saying in the moment, but I had gotten my special orders.

It happened only because I heard God's divine whisper.

THE CHANGE WITHIN

Discovering your unique life message is a wonderful thing. But it's not enough. You also need to discover the voice of God speaking into your life, giving you special orders for your message to make a difference in the world.

When we do that, it changes us. Hearing God's divine whisper produces a change in our attitudes and motivations, a switch from our own desires to responses of compassion and love. God's voice makes us sensitive to the needs of people around us.

A friend of ours was driving down the highway and came upon a pickup truck parked by the side of the road. An elderly man and woman stood beside it. One wheel was jacked up, and a tire leaned against the rear bumper.

My friend whizzed by in his car. But as he passed, he heard in his heart: *Stop. They have a flat tire, and the spare is flat.*

At first he kept going. But the farther he went, the heavier he felt, and the words kept repeating in his mind: *They have a flat, and the spare is flat.*

Finally he turned around and went back. When my friend got out and asked what was wrong, the man said, "Got a flat tire, and the spare is flat."

My friend gave the man a ride to a service station to get the tire fixed and then went back to tell the woman her husband would be along shortly. She smiled and said, "You're a Christian, aren't you?" My friend said yes. And she added, "I am too, and I was praying for help when you stopped."

Even though my friend didn't immediately stop, he was open enough to the whisper of God to hear it. He was able to hear God's whisper in the silence of his car. It tuned him in to the need of people he was passing by.

That was sacred silence.

Bill Hybels has said, "If you lower the ambient noise of your life and listen expectantly for those whispers of God, your ears will hear them. And when you follow their lead, your world will be rocked."[5]

That's what God can do when we're paying attention.

The Divine Whisper

1. Read Proverbs 3:5–7: "Trust in the LORD with all your heart and lean not on your own understanding; in all your ways submit to him, and he will make your paths straight. Do not be wise in your own eyes; fear the LORD and shun evil."

2. Try lectio divina. How do the four approaches to Scripture open up the Bible to you?

3. Spend five minutes in silence, and listen for God's "still small voice" (1 Kings 19:12, NKJV).

4. Pray about the decisions coming up in your day, and ask for God's guidance.

Love the One in Front of You

1. Ask God to open your eyes to see the needs of people right around you who are hurting.

2. Do something loving by listening to someone in your life and simply giving that person your undivided attention.

Your comfort zone is the death zone. God loves you enough to shove you out of your comfort zone and into your calling.

#BeTheMessage

7

Holy Disturbance

I saw a woman dying on the street outside Camp-
bell Hospital. I picked her up and took her to the
hospital, but she was refused admission, because
she was poor. She died on the street. I knew then
that I must make a home for the dying—a resting
place for people going to Heaven.

Mother Teresa

If you want to be a real human being...you can-
not tolerate things which put you to indignation,
to outrage. You must stand up.

Stéphane Hessel

Stéphane Hessel, a concentration-camp survivor and a member of the French Resistance, stood up against the Nazi regime of the 1930s and 1940s. His little book, titled *Time for Outrage,* sold more than four million copies in its day. He once said, "Look around; look at what makes you un-happy, what makes you furious, and then engage yourself in some action."[1]

If there's a time to be quiet and still so you can hear the whisper of God to direct you in your life message, then there's also a time to be aware of and frustrated by the evils and injustice in the world around you.

We call this "holy disturbance."

In order to find God's unique expression of His message in our lives, we need more than the uncomfortable guilt of being people born in a country of plenty. We need to do more than nod at the needs we see around us.

We need a divine disturbance that prompts us to action, gets us out of our comfort zones, and propels us into the place where God's calling is so obvious.

THE UNCOMFORTABLE ZONE

You'll recognize your unique holy disturbance. It's the issue that hits you like a kick in the gut. It's the news story that makes you see red, the troubling statistic that you're unable to forget, the television image that seems to be embedded on the inside of your eyelids.

It's the thing that bothers you enough to make you consider moving out of your comfort zone to become part of the solution.

Mother Teresa was moved by just such a disturbance.

In 1943 famine struck the Bengal province in India. British estimates suggest that as many as four million people starved to death. A few years later, in 1946, Muslim violence broke out in Calcutta. Thousands more died. A nun at the Loretto convent in Calcutta, who was then known as Sister Teresa, witnessed the misery those catastrophes brought to the people of the city, and her heart ached for them. She prayed often about how to respond but had no clear direction. But one day, while on a train returning from a weekend spiritual retreat, she felt a strong leading that she should leave the convent where she'd been working and minister to the poor of the city as one of them, begging for her own subsistence while loving the people of the slum.

Nothing about her prior experience would have indicated a personal source of physical or emotional pain that might have made her sensitive to poverty. There was nothing in her past to drive her toward hunger as a motivating issue. She was simply filled with sudden compassion and a certainty that God wanted her to help. Today, we refer to her as Mother Teresa because that's what she became to the poor and powerless of Calcutta, a mother.

The poor and powerless are mentioned nearly three thousand times in Scripture. It's simply not possible to read our Bibles for five minutes without coming face to face with God's fierce love for the poor and His intense passion for justice.

So, who are the poor?

If you have money in a bank account or in your wallet—in any amount—you're doing better than 92 percent of the world's population. You might not feel successful, and in fact, you might be genuinely financially stretched. Even so, if you have money in any amount, you are among the world's financial elite. And if you have the three essentials—food to eat, clothes to wear, and a place to sleep—you're better off than 75 percent of the world today. In other words, if you're reading this book, you're probably not among the billions of the world's poorest people.

The genuinely poor are cheated out of the opportunity to make their own choices. The needs they have are a laundry list of basic things we take for granted.

Safety. Violence robs the poor of the ability to protect themselves from criminals and sexual predators. Even if laws exist, local law enforcement often does not. In poor communities the local police may be so corrupt that they are people to run from, not to.

Clean drinking water and nutritious food. Twelve percent of the world's population uses 85 percent of its water, and none of the 12 percent live in developing countries. The absence of safe drinking water leaves the poor vulnerable to disease; 2.3 billion people are affected by waterborne diseases each year.

Medical care. The poor generally begin life at a disadvantage as underweight babies because they are born to malnourished mothers who received no prenatal care. Preventable health issues such as malaria, diarrhea, and pneumonia cause tens of thousands of deaths each day. Even the most basic medical care is unavailable or unaffordable for the poorest.

Education. The poor, especially girls, are often denied the opportunity to obtain a basic education. Compulsory school fees are commonplace in many countries and prevent poor children from gaining skills that could break the chains of poverty. The decision to obtain a safe, affordable education oftentimes simply isn't an option.

Worship. People need more than the ability to exist. They also need a reason to live. Millions of people across the globe live their entire lives without ever having the option of worshiping openly or owning a Bible.

In the words of Stéphane Hessel, why aren't we more outraged by the needs of the poor?

Maybe you can tell that this is Chris writing, and my personal holy disturbance is the unique pain and vulnerability of the poor. I was stunned as I saw the news reports roll in on January 12, 2010. An earthquake had caused unimaginable devastation in Haiti, the poorest country in the Western Hemisphere. The images of pancaked buildings, wounded adults, and crying children gave us a tiny glimpse of the despair the Haitians must have felt.

Something in me rose up. It was a holy disturbance. I knew I had to help.

To be honest with you, I have a love/hate relationship with my holy disturbance. Opening my eyes to the pain of the poor through television or online news reports is one thing. Engaging on a personal level—well, it hurts. It's certainly not comfortable or convenient.

I'd already spent quite a bit of time working in third-world countries. I'd sat in the huts of African villagers with hollow eyes suffering from endless, gnawing hunger. I'd held the hand of a twelve-year-old girl in Central America as she rocked her baby and shared a story of unspeakable horror. I'd stumbled through the rubble of Banda Aceh, Indonesia, while the stench of death from the 2004 tsunami filled the humid air.

So when I saw images from Haiti, I knew what getting involved there would take. At least I thought I knew.

After quickly assembling a missions team, gathering desperately needed medical supplies, and making flight arrangements, I flew from Houston, had a short layover in Miami, and landed in…hell. Nothing in my experience had prepared me for the reality I faced.

From the moment I stepped off the plane, I was surrounded by absolute, utter chaos. My senses were flooded by wailing mothers with empty arms, desperate children with nothing to eat, and new amputees with crudely wrapped stumps. The acrid smoke of burning rubber stung my nose, and the stench of raw sewage turned my stomach. Flies buzzed around my face. Mosquitoes whined in my ears. And everywhere I turned, I saw nothing but the empty faces of a people without hope.

Part of the purpose of that initial visit to Haiti was to find a place where we could invest for the long term in hopes of making a long-term difference. With that in mind we partnered with pastors and organizations in Port-au-Prince to discover where our strengths best addressed the needs of the Haitian people.

As we left the airport, I realized that every square foot that wasn't covered in rubble had sprouted misshapen tents. They dotted the landscape like an overgrowth of unwanted mushrooms. Not really tents but makeshift scraps of plastic, bits of wood, or anything else the people could find to provide some semblance of shade and privacy.

In the days that followed, we worked alongside Haitians from sunup to sundown providing assistance in any way we could. Much of our time was spent handing out bags of beans and rice. With each bag I did my best to offer a smile and the few awkward words I knew in Creole, but all the while I kept my emotions at arm's length. Our effort, as tenuous as it was, attracted a tide of pain that washed toward us each day. To wade through it, I intentionally disengaged my heart from my head, rationalizing that in that ravaged country I needed to make quick, efficient decisions that weren't muddied by emotion.

At night, however, it was harder to keep my emotions corralled. I would lie awake in the dark, alternating between cocooning my entire body and head in my sheet to stave off the mosquitoes, and throwing the sheet off my body to escape the oppressive heat. And all the while faces and stories of the day crowded my mind.

That system of heart management, stuffing down my emotions during the day and wrestling with them at night, worked well at first as I immersed myself in the mountain of details that faced us. But all of that changed when one of those statistics climbed up into my lap.

THE SILENT ONE

Earlier in the day we had overseen the cooking of rice and beans flavored with a few twiglike chicken bones. Then we sat through an intense meeting with other aid leaders. When the meeting was over, I wandered outside the building where we'd met, hoping the heat outside might be accompanied by a breeze.

Exhausted, I sat down on a rough plank supported by two stones, leaned my head back, and closed my eyes. Almost immediately I felt a tug, and my eyes popped open. A little boy who was no more than four or five, dressed in only a ragged T-shirt, climbed into my lap.

And into my heart.

He was clearly hungry and sick but didn't cry or make a sound. He just sat there, silently staring at me. I didn't speak Creole, and he didn't speak English, but I think there's a universal language between mothers and children, a silent one that's deeper and far more eloquent than clumsy spoken words.

I instinctively slipped my arms around him and began to rock gently back and forth. I tried to smile, to put on a pleasant face, but my heart was breaking. My tears began to flow.

Suddenly all those statistics exploded in my head as I thought about the 1.3 million Haitians who were living in tents. Three hundred thousand children—most of them just like the little boy I was holding—were orphaned with no one to look after them.

Three. Hundred. Thousand.

No foster care. No government agency handing out meals. No public housing. And none on the way either. Unless we did something to help, the little boy sitting on my lap and a myriad of others like him would live short, miserable lives and never know of love or hope. I felt so inadequate.

Faced with the sheer magnitude of Haiti's problems, I wanted to cry out to God. I got up from that bench crushed, yet somehow stronger. I realized that being efficient isn't necessarily the same thing as being effective. I reflected on the arrogance of my plan to protect my heart by not engaging emotionally with hurting Haitians. With great shame I realized that I had effectively been saying, "I'm sorry. Your pain just hurts me too much."

Things changed after that. I allowed myself to hurt with the hurting and discovered that I had found that special niche where my passion met their need. I did what I could. They needed food, shelter, and water, but they also needed to share their stories. This I could do; I could listen. I kept an interpreter at my side throughout the remainder of the trip and shared countless tears, hugs, and words of hope with new friends young and old.

Maybe you're thinking, *I get what you're saying about experiencing a holy disturbance. That's happened to me. And I would love to make a difference, but I'm just an everyday person, and most of the world's problems are systemic and complex.*

When we first hear about someone else's pain—whether it's news of a sick coworker, statistics of violence in an inner-city neighborhood, or a devastating natural disaster—our first reaction is usually something like, "Oh, that's awful. I feel so sorry for them." And our interaction ends there. It's not that we're apathetic; we're insecure about getting involved. We resist engagement because we're afraid—afraid of embarrassment, inconvenience, inexperience, and ineffectiveness. Inner voices take over:

I might say the wrong thing.

I don't know how to help.

No one's asked me to do anything.

I can't fix this.

I can't possibly make a difference.

That reaction is understandable. I've felt the debilitating frustration and hopelessness of insecurity more times than I can count. But, after traveling the globe working among the poor and powerless, I've finally come to realize a key truth: my insecurity is really a lack of confidence in God's ability. If God wants to do something, it doesn't matter what or whom He chooses to do it through. His power trumps everything.

THE POWER OF ONE

Reading 1 Samuel 13–14 helped me understand how God works in humanly impossible situations. It tells the story of a seemingly doomed battle and the difference that one person can make. The army of Israel had dwindled to six hundred men whose only weapons were two swords, two spears, and some dull farming tools.

On the other side of the valley was the Philistine army with three thousand chariots, six thousand cavalry, and a sea of foot soldiers holding razor-sharp swords and spears. Hmm…which side would you bet on?

Me too.

But one man dared to believe that God could do whatever He wanted with whomever He chose—and dared to believe that person could be him.

Jonathan, a soldier in the Israelite army and a son of the king, looked across the valley at a sea of enemies armed to the teeth. Then he looked behind him at his ragtag, ill-equipped comrades. His response to that grim situation shattered every excuse we could ever offer to resist engagement. Instead of retreating in fear, Jonathan boldly turned to his armorbearer and said, "Come, let's go.… Perhaps the LORD will act in our behalf. Nothing can hinder the LORD from saving, whether by many or by few" (14:6).

One thing is clear: Jonathan had complete confidence in the Lord's power to save. His courage wasn't the result of his own ability. It was exactly the opposite. Jonathan's courage came from the knowledge that God didn't need him to accomplish anything. He understood that God wanted to crush evil and rescue Israel from the Philistines. He said, "Come, let's go," because he refused to miss the chance of being used by God. It wasn't enough to just believe that God could do it. Jonathan had to act on his confidence.

Without telling anyone, Jonathan and his armorbearer headed toward the Philistine army and attacked. Much to everyone's surprise, confusion ensued, and the panicked Philistines began fighting among themselves. At the end of the day, the decimated Philistine army was defeated, and those who were still able to flee turned and ran.

The unthinkable had happened. God had rescued the army of Israel.

When you experience a holy disturbance, you always have a choice. You can shrink back in insecurity or step forward in complete confidence that God is able to overcome against all odds—and that you're the one He might choose as the means to accomplish victory.

Doubting God's ability to use your unique life message is to doubt God's ability. Do you believe that the Lord can save "by many or by few"? If so, why not you?

Consider your reaction carefully; it's audacious to think that our personal limitations can actually inhibit God's ability. In fact, Scripture tells us that the opposite is true. God chooses to work through our weaknesses. God said, "My grace is all you need. My power works best in weakness" (2 Corinthians 12:9, NLT).

Who are we to say that God can't use us, that we're too weak?

You see, we simply can't have it both ways. We can't claim that God is all powerful and also believe that He's unable to overcome in a situation with people like us. Either both statements are true, or both are false.

As uncomfortable as it might make us feel, the truth is that God is able to do anything, and that includes using you and me to be His message to a hurting world.

HOLY DISTURBANCE IN ACTION

Several years ago we added a bookstore and café to our church campus. This made it much easier for members of our congregation and people from the community to purchase Christian books and Bibles. It also provided a great environment to gather with friends and colleagues.

But not long after we opened the shop, I felt a holy disturbance each time I entered it. The shelves were stocked with many useful and wonderful books, and Bibles were readily available—all of which was very important to me and served a helpful purpose—but something wasn't right. The bookstore was proclaiming many messages, but it wasn't being the message.

I reviewed our use of space and realized far too much of the area was devoted to the sale of Christian gifts and accessories. Gifts and accessories are not intrinsically bad items for a store to carry, but as the percentage of space devoted to those items became obvious, I knew we needed to change our product mix and use the space in a way that made a real difference in the world, rather than merely functioning as a retail outlet.

After a little more soul-searching and prayer, we decided to convert the bookstore from a traditional Christian retail model to a fair-trade store. One that carried products made by people living in foreign countries to whom we ministered. A location that would connect our people to believers in other parts of the world who were struggling to escape challenging and often life-threatening circumstances.

As great as that idea seemed, I procrastinated and put off redoing the space, thinking, *I have so many other things to do. I'll get to the bookstore sometime later.* But God wouldn't leave me alone about it. My holy disturbance wouldn't go away, nor would it be set aside.

Over the next several months the disturbance in my spirit grew stronger. When I finally surrendered to the leading of the Lord and explained the concept to our team, they were excited to do something with the space that actually mattered. The holy disturbance I experienced turned into a holy excitement for them as God moved in our hearts.

A few months later, by the grace of God and the hard work of our staff and volunteers, the bookstore reopened as one of the largest fair-trade and direct-trade stores in the country. Through it, our members and customers obtain unique, well-made products. Money from those purchases provides a living for the craftsmen who created those items and brings new opportunities to their families. In turn, the store's profits go back into our ministry and missions. We still carry Christian books and Bibles, but most of the shelves are stocked with fair-trade and direct-trade products.

One of the people transformed through this effort is Jhuma, a woman who lives in India. When she was ten years old, a well-dressed man came to her village promising parents that he would give their children a good education in the city and provide jobs for them when they came of age. Wanting better lives for their children, many in the village were duped by him and agreed to send their children to live with him. Jhuma and her sisters were among those children.

Once in the city, the girls were separated from each other. Jhuma was locked in a room with only a single bed. She sat on the bed and cried, not knowing where she was or what would happen to her. Before long, she heard the keys rattle in the lock on the door, and a strange man entered the room. What followed was her introduction to the life of forced prostitution.

Eight years later Jhuma met a woman who told her about Jesus and offered her a chance to escape. Jhuma seized that opportunity. Free at last, she went to work for the woman who rescued her, making blankets from used saris. Those blankets are now one of the best-selling items in our fair-trade store. Jhuma can now make a decent wage as people from our church and community buy her beautiful blankets. We have found that those who live in poverty aren't looking for a handout but for an opportunity.

Profits we make from Jhuma's blankets and from the sale of other items allow us to help others like Njah, a pottery maker who lives in the small African village of Bamessing in northwest Cameroon. He learned his craft from his mother, who has been a member of an artisan's co-op for more than forty years. We sell Njah's unbelievably beautiful pottery in our store. The income he receives from those sales is important to his entire family. He is now their sole wage earner. Beyond paying for the basic necessities of food and shelter, his work also covers the school fees for his sister and niece, which opens the door of opportunity for them as well.

Hundreds of disadvantaged handicraft artisans like Njah and his mother have become self-reliant through the sale of their products in international markets like ours. Profitable co-ops similar to theirs stem the flow of people from rural areas into the cities, strengthen the integrity of families and marriages, preserve traditional crafts and cultural heritage, and instill self-confidence in their members.

Another of those helped in this way is Catherine, who lives in the slums of Nairobi, Kenya. A single mother with a two-year-old daughter, she struggled daily to find food and shelter. So when someone offered to provide a meal and a place to sleep for a night, she was glad to accept it. That turned out to be the worst decision of her life.

That night she was raped and as a result became pregnant. Later she learned she'd also become HIV positive. Sick, pregnant, unemployed, and homeless, Catherine was desperate to end her life. The only thing that stopped her was the thought of leaving her daughter without a mother.

But while living on the street, she and her children were noticed by a woman named Lillian. Lillian told Catherine that she mattered to God, invited her to accept Jesus as her Savior, and introduced her to a new family—Woodlands Church, Nairobi. With the help of her new family, Catherine learned skills that allow her to earn a living. Now she makes handbags, jewelry, and other items and uses the income to provide housing, food, clothing, and security for her family.

On one of my visits to our church plant in the Kware Slum outside of Nairobi, I had the privilege of going to Catherine's home. There I saw for the first time the amazing handbags that she made. Immediately God spoke to my heart and prompted me to tell Catherine that we wanted to buy all the handbags she had so we could sell them in our store. I'll never forget the look on her face when she realized that someone had noticed her brilliant work.

Tears filled Catherine's eyes as she hugged me and told me, "Now I can afford the medicine for my HIV. Asante sana!"

Many people in our church who could never travel to Kenya to meet and minister to Catherine have made a huge difference in her life by purchasing her beautiful handbags.

At the age of eight, Eden, a young girl from Ethiopia, experienced the tragic loss of her father. Worried about her family and responsible for supporting her widowed mother, Eden started working as a prostitute. She worked for more than sixteen years on the streets, where she was bought and sold as a commodity.[2]

She wanted a fresh start but could never find work. With no education and no other options, Eden was forced to remain in prostitution. One day she met a group of women from a co-op of skilled artisans who gave her that opportunity.

After receiving training, Eden began creating leather goods, scarves, and other handmade items. Her new venture into self-employment has restored her joy, hope, and sense of value. By purchasing their craft items, we empower Eden and other women like her to break the chains of prostitution.

Each of these lives was transformed because God led us and others working in ministry to the powerless and poor through a holy disturbance—an unsettling so deep and persistent in our spirits that we were compelled to act. And not just a single disturbance or a single response, but many disturbances and responses at each stage of the work, from rescue to sustainable lifestyles.

Responding to those disturbances wasn't always easy, and it wasn't always comfortable, but the results God was able to bring made all of it worth the effort, an effort that continues even now.

What Is Your Holy Disturbance?

I really like a prayer Craig Groeschel wrote:

> May God bless you with discomfort at easy answers, half truths, and superficial relationships, so that you may live deep within your heart.
>
> May God bless you with anger at injustice, oppression, and the exploitation of people, so that you may work for justice, freedom, and peace.
>
> May God bless you with tears to shed for those who suffer from pain, rejection, and starvation, so that you may reach out your hand to comfort them and to turn their pain into joy.
>
> And may God bless you with enough foolishness to believe that you can make a difference in this world, so that you can do what others claim cannot be done....
>
> Amen.[3]

A holy disturbance isn't necessarily a big thing.

It doesn't have to be about revamping bookstores or going to Haiti. It might be about a need in your neighborhood, a friend's predicament, or something that's being overlooked or neglected in your town or at your office. A holy disturbance is simply anything that troubles you because of the way it affects another person—whatever violates your sense of justice or touches your heart.

It's something that becomes so unsettling you feel compelled to act.

The "holy" in "holy disturbance" is God writing His message on your life. It is your willingness to act in the direction of being the gospel. It is your making something happen by being the hands and feet of Jesus in the world.

So what's God pointing out to you? What's your holy disturbance?

What are you waiting for?

The Divine Whisper

1. Pray. Ask God to reveal to you your holy disturbance.

2. Read Matthew 25:35–40: "'For I was hungry and you gave me something to eat, I was thirsty and you gave me something to drink, I was a stranger and you invited me in, I needed clothes and you clothed me, I was sick and you looked after me, I was in prison and you came to visit me.' Then the righteous will answer him, 'Lord, when did we see you hungry and feed you, or thirsty and give you something to drink? When did we see you a stranger and invite you in, or needing clothes and clothe you? When did we see you sick or in prison and go to visit you?' The King will reply, 'Truly I tell you, whatever you did for one of the least of these brothers and sisters of mine, you did for me.'"

3. Mother Teresa once said, "The poor are Jesus in disguise." Ask God to open your eyes to "the least of these" all around you.

4. Spend five minutes in silence letting Christ fill you with the excitement of His calling on your life.

Love the One in Front of You

1. Remember that everyone you meet has a hidden hurt. Stop long enough to hear the hurt, and take an action step to help.

2. Sign up for a missions project at your church, or start a new one in your neighborhood. Remember you don't have to go to the other side of the world to be the message. There are countless opportunities to serve the poor and powerless all around you. Here are a few suggestions:
   - homeless shelters
   - feeding programs for the hungry
   - mentoring and reading programs for at-risk kids

- pregnancy-assistance programs that give unwed mothers the help and love they need so they don't terminate the pregnancy but make the baby available for adoption (The unborn are truly "the least of these" because they have no voice.)

Part 3

Understanding...

The Message That Confounds the World

As we think about taking our life message into the world, whether to the neighbor next-door or the couple downtown or a family across the ocean, we need to understand what the world really is. More to the point, *who* the world really is.

As Christians, we often talk about the world in terms of us versus them. We tend to separate ourselves from the world and look across that separation at "them." We see the world as antagonistic to our message and the gospel.

And there is some truth in that. As followers of Jesus, we deeply believe certain absolutes based on the authority of the Bible, and sometimes the world around us—governments, organizations, people groups—defies those beliefs. In those circumstances we feel it's important to stand for what we hold true. We find ourselves at odds with the culture of the day, and things inevitably become us versus them.

I get that, but more and more, I think differently about this "world" we talk about. In fact, the message of the gospel is that we are *all* sinners. As we've already discussed, the source of our deepest and most powerful life message is our own brokenness and the amazing transformation that comes from redemption. That's where our life message and the gospel intersect.

Our perspective on the world should not be us versus them but rather us *and* them. If we come at this any other way, our message will be kept at arm's length, and we will be separated from the very people we are trying to connect with.

I know this sounds simplistic, but I think it's true. The world consists of two kinds of people: those who are *skeptics* and those who are *thirsty*.

Some people are just flat-out skeptics. The Bible describes them this way: "They are darkened in their understanding and separated from the life of God because of the ignorance that is in them due to the hardening of their hearts" (Ephesians 4:18). You will encounter people, even next-door, who will reject your life message and the gospel you carry to them, but we need to remember that at one time or another, we were skeptics too. We've all had doubts and questions.

We need to understand that both skeptical people and thirsty people need the same gospel we carry. We may be at odds with what skeptics in the world believe, but we often need to lay down our verbal swords and extend our loving hands. It's usually not words but actions that speak the loudest. Your life message should be not so much about debate but love.

And those who are thirsty are not only those living in third-world countries; many are living next-door or down the street. Thirst can be physical, spiritual, or both. Often as we provide for someone's physical needs, the person is drinking from our pitchers of spiritual water as well.

I've come to think that as our lives carry the gospel into the world, we sometimes worry too much and try too hard.

That's because the task of being the message can be daunting, scary, and uncomfortable. We're all afraid of rejection. We all fear being inadequate in living out the message to others.

You, right now, may be hesitant about being the message because of this very thing.

Relax. There's something you have that you may not be aware of. It's the innate power of the gospel. The apostle Paul testified to this: "And so it was with me, brothers and sisters. When I came to you, I did not come with eloquence or human wisdom as I proclaimed to you the testimony about God. For I resolved to know nothing while I was with you except Jesus Christ and him crucified. I came to you in weakness with great fear and trembling. My message and my preaching were not with wise and persuasive words, but with a demonstration of the Spirit's power, so that your faith might not rest on human wisdom, but on God's power" (1 Corinthians 2:1–5).

The power of the gospel will shine through your life message in the world. It is not about coming up with wise and persuasive words to convince the hardened skeptic, but rather about the power of the Spirit in your life to come alongside the skeptic and serve the thirsty.

You see, the message we carry to the world has innate, incomprehensible power.

All God asks of you is to *be*. To be the message. To be the gospel. The power of the gospel will do the rest.

The world has no explanation
for a life transformed by the
power of Christ. A changed life
is proof God is alive.

#BeTheMessage

The Message the World Has No Explanation For

> *But God hath chosen the foolish things of the*
> *world to confound the wise; and God hath chosen*
> *the weak things of the world to confound the*
> *things which are mighty.*
>
> 1 Corinthians 1:27, KJV

> *The voice of sin is loud, but the voice of*
> *forgiveness is louder.*
>
> D. L. Moody

There are three characteristics of a gospel-filled life, three dimensions to your life message, that will utterly confound the world around you.

To the skeptic, each of these three is puzzling and often without retort or comeback. To the thirsty, each of these three is compelling, refreshing, and thirst quenching.

The three come, free of charge, with the gospel: truth, love, and grace.

TRUTH UNEXPECTED

One thing that always surprises the world is truth.

I don't mean telling the truth, although that's part of it. I don't mean integrity, although that too is part of it. And I don't mean just generally being an honest person, although, again, that's a good thing to be.

I'm talking about the truth of a life. The truth of a life transformed. The truth of your life turned around. That becomes the power of your life message, the message of truth that the world never really expects.

In 1973 Chuck Colson was special counsel to the president of the United States. He was also known as the White House hatchet man and the "evil genius" of Richard Nixon's administration.[1] Colson intentionally spread false information regarding Daniel Ellsberg, of Pentagon Papers fame, in order to discredit him politically. He also proposed a plan to have the Brookings Institution firebombed in order to create a distraction from the growing media interest in the Watergate break-in.

His specialty was underhanded political dirty tricks designed to smear and damage political opponents. He was really good at distorting the truth. In fact, a former marine, Colson described himself as someone "valuable to the President...because I was willing...to be ruthless in getting things done."[2]

This was, at that time, his life message.

In March of 1974, Chuck Colson was indicted for his role in the conspiracy to cover up the Watergate burglaries. He was found guilty of obstruction of justice and was sentenced to serve one to three years in prison.

But just before he entered prison, he was given a copy of C. S. Lewis's *Mere Christianity*, a classic work that makes a clear, simple argument in defense of the claim that Jesus was indeed who He said He was—the Christ, the Messiah, the Son of the living God.

That book changed his life. It turned him around. Chuck Colson gave his life to Jesus Christ.

He would later write, "I know the resurrection is a fact, and Watergate proved it to me. How? Because twelve men testified they had seen Jesus raised from the dead, then they proclaimed that truth for forty years, never once denying it. Every one was beaten, tortured, stoned and put in prison. They would not have endured that if it weren't true. Watergate embroiled twelve of the most powerful men in the world—and they couldn't keep a lie for three weeks. You're telling me twelve apostles could keep a lie for forty years? Absolutely impossible."[3]

Colson served his time in prison, an experience that would shape his future life message. Understanding the hearts and souls of men behind bars equipped him in a unique way. He now had a heavy heart for the thirsty, and he had the living water of the gospel to offer them.

A year after his release, in 1976, Colson founded Prison Fellowship, a ministry built on his unique life message that would be the gospel to people behind bars. Colson soon became a prominent Christian leader in the church, in culture, and throughout the world, as well as an author of dozens of books that would deeply influence people's lives.

But his real legacy, the truth of his life, was found in his many visitations with prisoners, his engagement with ex-cons trying to rebuild their lives, and his tireless compassion for those whose lives of doing wrong, just like his, became transformed by the message of the gospel.

Yet throughout his life, despite his thirty-six years of ministering to people behind bars, cynics sniped that Colson was a fraud, that he had dodged a fuller justice in 1975, and that his transformation couldn't possibly be real. You see, skeptics didn't know what to do with Chuck Colson's life transformation. They had no answer for the truth of his life. Even though Colson devoted his later life to people behind bars, the truth of his life was unexpected and too hard for them to believe.

The world has no explanation for a transformed life. It doesn't believe there's anything on earth that can turn a life from self-centeredness and power hunger to tireless devotion to people in prison. And the world is right. Nothing *on earth* can cause that change, that transformation.

But God can.

Let me tell you also about Robert Sutton.

He was a lost man. Lost in crime. Lost in the prison system. As a teen, he'd been active in the drug scene and involved in gangs in Houston. Eventually convicted for committing murder, Robert was sentenced to thirty-five years in a Texas prison.

In 1997, behind bars, Sutton applied for a prison program called IFI. InnerChange Freedom Initiative teaches inmates about personal responsibility and the rippling effects of one's crimes through others' lives. IFI turned Sutton's life around. He would say later that he experienced freedom while still behind bars. Robert Sutton was a thirsty man. Thirsty for something more in his life.

IFI was, and is, a prison values program started by Chuck Colson.

Sutton said that through IFI, "I was taught that even though my body was confined, my mind and spirit could be freed through Jesus Christ."[4] Sutton ultimately served thirteen years of his sentence, was released in 1998, and went to work on staff at a church in Houston, Texas.

The truth of Chuck Colson's life was dismissed by skeptics. It was unexpected and therefore incomprehensible. Yet for a thirsty man like Robert Sutton, the truth of Colson's life offered freedom and living water.

You and I may not have a life message as dramatic as Chuck Colson's, but we do have a unique life message molded in our own pain and brokenness. That message carries with it the truth of our lives. Do not underestimate the power of that truth. Sure, some will be cynical and dismissive. Then again, they may in time be overwhelmed by the gospel lived out. And there are always those who are thirsty.

Your life can and will, by God's grace, touch them all, often in ways you will never know.

LOVE INCOMPREHENSIBLE

One of the great love stories of all time is in the Old Testament, the story of Hosea and Gomer.

Hosea was a prophet to Israel in a time of prosperity. The spiritual problem of the time was idolatry and moral laxity. As the people of Israel had begun to adopt idols from other nations' religions, their own sexual behaviors had started to slide. The role of prophet in that day was often to be the voice of conscience to a nation, so Hosea's job was to call Israel to task regarding their immorality.

A thankless task.

God directed Hosea's life to become a mirror of His own love for the idol-worshiping Israelites. He instructed Hosea to take a wife, specifically "a wife of harlotry" (Hosea 1:2, NKJV). We don't know the details, but Gomer apparently had a loose moral background. Nonetheless, perhaps she found herself attracted to the moral strength of the young preacher Hosea. Maybe Hosea represented the possibility of a virtuous life.

Again, we don't know the details of their relationship. But the Bible tells us they got married and their early marriage blossomed. They even had a child together, a son named Jezreel.

But over time Gomer became restless. She lost interest in Hosea. She spent more time away from home. Soon Gomer became pregnant again and bore another child, this time a girl.

Hosea's heart was breaking because he knew the child was not his, nor was a third child, a son. Gomer's infidelity became clear to everyone.

Yet Hosea remained faithful to her. Each time that she would leave home and then return, he would take her back. Over and over Gomer left to be with someone else and then returned to Hosea's still-loving arms.

Ultimately Gomer let Hosea know she was leaving for good to be with her lover. She chose her life of sin over the life message and constant love of Hosea. She left, despite his protests, and Hosea remained home, caring for the children. Despite her terrible treatment of him and her infidelity, Hosea longed for her and still loved her deeply.

In time it was learned that Gomer's lover had deserted her, and she had sold herself into sexual slavery. She had hit bottom.

No one would blame Hosea for moving on with his life. For most anyone that would have certainly been the end.

But no.

Against all odds Hosea still loved her. God instructed him, "Go again, love a woman who is loved by her husband, yet an adulteress, even as the LORD loves the sons of Israel, though they turn to other gods" (Hosea 3:1, NASB). God told Hosea to find her and rescue her from her sad and hopeless life.

Today we rightly ask the question, "Where does that kind of love come from?" The answer is in that same verse: "even as the LORD loves the sons of Israel." As followers of Christ, we have the kind of love that God imparts to us, a love that is incomprehensible to the world.

And incomprehensible to Hosea's friends.

Hosea searched for Gomer, seeking to find the love of his life wherever and in whatever state she might be. Once he found her, Hosea bought Gomer out of her sexual slavery (what an image of unconditional love!) and brought her home again to live with him.

To a skeptic, this truly is incomprehensible and likely to be dismissed as a Bible fairy tale. To someone who is thirsty, it brings tears. You see, all of us who are or have been thirsty in our lives see ourselves as Gomer, that one who has sinned again and again, who has made a mess of everything, and who has turned her back on the only one who truly loved her.

C. S. Lewis wrote a book titled *The Four Loves*. In it he suggests the four types of love are affection, friendship, romance, and charity. The last one—charity (sometimes called agape)—is unconditional love, the love that comes from God, who is love. It's love we don't deserve. The other three loves are natural types of love that we are born with. Agape love, charity, is the supernatural love given to us by God Himself.

This is the kind of love that confounds the world. It's illustrated well by a simple story I heard of a grandfather and his grandson. The grandfather found his grandson, Tanner, jumping up and down in his playpen, crying at the top of his voice. When Tanner saw his grandfather, he reached up his little chubby hands and, crying, said, "Out, Gramp, out."

It was only natural for Gramp to reach down to lift the little fellow out of his predicament. But as he was doing so, the mother of the child stepped up and said, "No, Tanner, you are being punished, so you must stay in."

The grandfather was at a loss to know what to do. The child's tears and chubby hands reached deep into his heart, but the mother's firmness in correcting her son for misbehavior must not be taken lightly. Here was a problem of love versus law.

But love found a way.

The grandfather could not take the youngster out of the playpen, so he crawled in with him.

The gospel is about God crawling in with us. Through Jesus's entering into our world and suffering for our messes, we encounter a love we've never known before, a love that becomes a part of us, a part of our life message.

Just as Hosea was a living symbol of God's love for Israel, so you are a living symbol of Christ's love for all of us. Just as Hosea's love story became his life message—not a love story he told but a love story he lived—so too our life message is the love story of us and God doing life together.

The Bible makes the same connection: "This is how we know what love is: Jesus Christ laid down his life for us. And we ought to lay down our lives for our brothers and sisters" (1 John 3:16). Christ's sacrificial love for us becomes our sacrificial love for others. He crawls in with us.

And we need to crawl in with others.

There's yet another example of love that the world has no answer for.

Ultimately when your life message is put into action, it forces the world to wrestle with a profound question: What makes someone do something good for a stranger? For a world that claims everything revolves around Self, what can possibly explain the phenomenon of people helping others they don't even know?

A woman in Toronto, Erin Koen, tells her own discovery of such love.

One afternoon she stumbled upon a magazine story that touched her deeply. It was about children in a hospital in Romania. She saw a picture of a young girl who was disabled, being held in the arms of a woman.

Erin compared herself to the girl in the picture. Erin was raised by a loving mother and father, always had plenty to eat, and had lived in a comfortable home. She reflected on family vacations and holidays with grandparents. She had grown up with so much. This girl had so little.

Looking again at the magazine picture, Erin couldn't help but focus on the woman who held the disabled girl. The woman was smiling, her eyes were happy, and she seemed so fully in love with the girl she held in her arms. What struck Erin was that this girl was not the woman's own child. Yet the love she showed was deep and genuine and full. It was, Erin writes, "a mother's love. A love that in Greek is referred to as Agape…unconditional love."

The magazine article talked about the hundreds of children in Bucharest who had been abandoned by their parents and overlooked by society. Admittedly, some parents were too poor to provide for their children and had decided that leaving them at the hospital gave the children their best chance to survive. Other children had been left without parents and without homes in a communistic country where generations of Romanians had been forced to live desperate lives.

This single magazine article and this image of a woman's joy in holding a child not her own moved Erin to radically change her life. By the next year she had raised funds to finance a trip to Romania. She became connected to an organization called ROCK—Reaching Out to Christ's Kids. And she soon met the beautiful woman pictured in the magazine article, a Mexican American named Nannette.

Nannette had come to Romania as a young missionary and had learned the Romanian language. She dearly loved these children in the hospital and worked tirelessly to care for them. She lived alone and received no financial reward for her services. There was no explanation for the sacrificial love of a woman like Nannette other than agape love.

Erin says, "I watched as Nannette treated every single child like it was her own. She loved on them and helped to give them the sense of security and safety."

That love not only changed those children's lives. It changed Erin's as well. She went on to assist with children's development programs in five other countries. She met her husband in South Africa, and now they have two children of their own.[5]

How can you comprehend the love of a woman like Nannette, who so unconditionally loves babies not her own? How can you explain the power of Nannette's life message to utterly transform the life of Erin, the writer of this precious story?

Well, you can't. When your life is a message of love to the world, there is no earthly explanation.

Skeptics will see this love, realize it's incomprehensible, and find ways to dismiss it.

The thirsty will see this love, deem it incomprehensible—and drink.

GRACE UNEXPLAINABLE

It's hard to imagine a more peaceful place in the United States than the Amish farmlands of Lancaster County, Pennsylvania. However, the serenity of this close-knit community was shattered on October 2, 2006, when a lone gunman entered an Amish schoolhouse and shot ten girls, ages six through thirteen, before turning the gun on himself.

When the details of the shooting began to emerge, it was learned that the shooter was a milk-truck driver named Charles Roberts. Roberts had been in the community for years and was even recognized by some of the children.

Roberts had entered the school carrying guns and yelling, "I'm angry at God, and I need to punish some Christian girls to get even with him."[6] Investigators would later find that years earlier Roberts and his wife, Marie, had a daughter who died shortly after birth. Apparently he had been deeply affected by the loss, and his mental state began to deteriorate shortly after.

The shooting sent shock waves across our nation as we had to come to grips with the fact that no community was safe from senseless violence. But an even greater shock wave was sent by the Amish community in Lancaster County when they demonstrated to the nation the incomprehensible power of forgiveness and grace.

It started when the grandfather of one of the girls who was killed expressed forgiveness for the shooter, Charles Roberts. Then to everyone's surprise, many Amish members of the community attended Roberts's funeral to comfort his wife and family, who were also dealing with unimaginable grief and confusion.

Marie Roberts would later express to reporters her shock and eternal gratitude for the genuine comfort she and her children received from the Amish families whose own children had been murdered by her husband.

This, my friend, is incomprehensible grace.

Nothing can explain it.

THE CROSS OR KARMA

The word *karma* originated in ancient India, and it simply means "action, work, or deed." Of course, Hinduism, Buddhism, and Eastern mysticism use the word *karma* to describe one of the main tenets in their religion. Karma is the teaching that your present deeds and actions always come back to influence your future. That is, good deeds contribute to good karma and future happiness, while bad deeds contribute to bad karma and future suffering.

A lot of people think the law of karma is only in Eastern religions, but did you know the Bible says karma is a universal law? Galatians 6:7 says, "Do not be deceived, God is not mocked; for whatever a man sows, that he will also reap" (NKJV).

So karma is real. It's what the Bible calls "reaping what you sow." It says that you get what you deserve. The problem for us is that we've all sinned, we all have done wrong things, and karma rightfully says that we all deserve future punishment. Eastern religions just compound the problem by saying the answer is just to get to a level where you always do good things and never sin. That only adds more guilt and a heavier burden.

Then grace breaks through!

Bono, the lead singer of U2, put it this way in an interview several years ago:

The thing that keeps me on my knees is the difference between Grace and Karma....

You see, at the center of all religions is the idea of Karma. You know, what you put out comes back to you: an eye for an eye, a tooth for a tooth, or in physics—in physical laws—every action is met by an equal or an opposite one. It's clear to me that Karma is at the very heart of the Universe. I'm absolutely sure of it. And yet, along comes this idea called Grace to upend all that.... Grace defies reason and logic. Love interrupts...the consequences of your actions, which in my case is very good news indeed, because I've done a lot of stupid stuff....

I'm holding out that Jesus took my sins onto the Cross, because I know who I am, and I hope I don't have to depend on my own religiosity.[7]

As Bono said, "Grace defies reason and logic." Karma is a concept that makes sense to skeptics. Grace is a concept that skeptics have no explanation for.

Jesus's disciples were baffled too. Remember when Peter approached Jesus and asked, "Lord, how often should I forgive someone who sins against me? Seven times?"

"No, not seven times," Jesus replied, "but seventy times seven" (Matthew 18:21–22, NLT).

According to Jewish law, a person was required to forgive someone three times.[8] So Peter had doubled it and was adding one more for good measure. He was trying to impress Jesus.

But Jesus said, "No,...seventy times seven."

Peter was astounded. The others with him were astonished. Seventy times seven? They must have been thinking, *That level of grace doesn't make any sense!*

But Jesus was saying to forgive others to infinity and beyond. He was saying we must consistently make our life message one of forgiveness and grace. He was saying that the power of grace is exponential.

And exponentially confounding to the world.

In my journey to embrace my life message, this understanding about the power of grace has led me to discover three things.

First, *grace is a gift that heals the giver.* I don't know if the members of that Amish community were conscious of this truth, but in their obedience to the gospel, they lived it out. By giving comfort to Marie and her children and extending grace and forgiveness to them, the Amish families were beginning the process of healing within themselves. (Who knows what might have happened had Charlie Roberts, years earlier in the aftermath of his newborn daughter's death, come to extend forgiveness to others for her death—to the doctors, the circumstances, even God Himself?)

Through grace we know that whether or not someone deserves forgiveness, by offering it, we become free. Taking the risk of forgiving others is the only way to find that freedom. For our own sake we have to risk extending the hand of forgiveness to those who've hurt us. Otherwise we'll remain trapped in bitterness and resentment, which might feel comfortable at first, but they can't change the past. All they can do is mess up the present.

Second, *grace is a choice that changes others and changes us.* Jesus's response to Peter about forgiveness was a stunning statement in itself, but He didn't stop there. He also said, "Do good to those who hate you, bless those who curse you, pray for those who mistreat you" (Luke 6:27–28).

Of course, this is the opposite of what the world tells us to do. The world says that when we're hurt, we should get even. Jesus says that when we get hurt, we should bless those who hurt us.

"Hold it," the world says. "That doesn't make any sense!"

No, it doesn't. And that's it exactly: true grace has no explanation, which is why when we extend grace to others, it confounds the world. And in its speechlessness, the world often changes. The cynic may soften. The thirsty may reach out for more living water.

So we should do good to those who offend us, bless those who speak ill of us, and pray for those who mistreat us. None of those is easy to do, but when we do all three of them together, our situations and relationships can be radically transformed. And even if our circumstances don't change, *we* can be transformed.

Of all the things Jesus told us to do, praying for the people who have offended us can be the most difficult. It's also the best measure of whether we've actually forgiven them.

When you pray for those who have hurt you, try to let that prayer reach at least as deep as the pain, asking God to do a work in the life of the offender that addresses the root of the problem. That's the kind of prayer Jesus is talking about when He says to pray for those who mistreat us. Right now you might be thinking of someone who has offended you very deeply, and all you can say is, "Are you kidding? I was deeply hurt. How in the world can I pray for that person?"

You can't do this on your own or with your own strength. It's impossible. But you can do it with Christ's power and by choosing to forgive. Forgiveness is not a feeling. No one ever feels like forgiving. Forgiveness is a choice, a decision. That's why Jesus said we should forgive seventy times seven. He was saying we are to forgive them now, before they ask, and later, after they ask. And He was saying we should forgive them every time after that when the hurt comes to mind.

We are to choose forgiveness. If we don't, we are destined to live a bitter life.

Bitterness is a poison, and forgiveness is the only antidote. When you hold on to your hurt, it turns into hatred and seeps into your other relationships, tainting them with the bitterness that grips your soul. It's time, today, to let go of your pain and release your offender so you can be set free from that person and give God greater control over your life.

Third, *grace offers the world a true portrait of Jesus.* If we don't learn how to forgive like Jesus, we really can't become like Jesus. If we don't learn the principle of forgiveness, we can't be the message to anyone, because that forgiveness—grace—is the message.

Leonardo da Vinci, one of the most famous artists in history, created a painting in a church in Milan famously known as *The Last Supper.* It, of course, depicts Jesus's dining with the disciples the night before He was crucified.

There are many fables and rumors surrounding the painting and at least one concerning da Vinci's depiction of Judas. According to one story, when da Vinci worked on *The Last Supper,* he was bitter toward a fellow painter who had offended him. As he painted his way through the scene of Jesus with the disciples, he came to the figure of Judas Iscariot. Thinking he would get even with the guy who'd offended him, da Vinci supposedly painted that fellow's face as the face of Judas. Doing that gave da Vinci a sense of satisfaction as he thought about all the people who would see that face, many of whom would recognize it.

However, when da Vinci came to paint the face of Christ, he struggled to get it right.

He tried several times to make things work, but nothing suited him. As he thought about why he was having such difficulty with it, he remembered the way he felt toward the man whose face he'd used for Judas Iscariot. Thinking of that, he realized the bitterness he harbored was affecting his own ability to paint. So he went to that man and forgave him, then came back and changed the face of Judas.

After that, he was able to paint the face of Christ.

Jesus forgave us, and we offer that forgiveness to others. When we grasp the power of grace, we start to paint a picture of Jesus to the world.

The life message of that Amish community shouted. This picture of extreme violence done to innocent people who responded with simple forgiveness was a message that painted a picture of Jesus to the world.

That message, and that Person, is utterly and beautifully confounding.

The Divine Whisper

1. Pray, asking God to fill you with His grace and truth.

2. Read John 1:14 again, and meditate on the fact that Jesus Christ was the fullness of grace and truth: "The Word became flesh and made his dwelling among us. We have seen his glory, the glory of the one and only Son, who came from the Father, full of grace and truth."

3. Spend five minutes in silence letting Christ fill you up with His grace and truth.

Love the One in Front of You

1. Is there anyone you need to forgive? Choose to forgive the person whether you feel like it or not. Forgive him or her for your own sake.

2. Pray for the person you forgave, and feel the burden of bitterness lift from your soul.

The message of Christ doesn't
relate to the culture;
it revolutionizes the culture.

#BeTheMessage

9

The Person the World Has No Explanation For

Grace is a person. And his name is Jesus.
Judah Smith

He's indescribable. He's incomprehensible. He's invincible. He's irresistible.... You can't outlive Him, and you can't live without Him.... That's my King!
S. M. Lockridge

When Jesus was crucified, two other men were put to death beside Him.

The Bible describes these men using different words: thieves, rebels, bad men, and criminals. But I would use two other words. One criminal was a skeptic. The other criminal was thirsty.

The skeptic taunted Jesus. "Aren't you the Messiah? Save yourself and us!" (Luke 23:39).

The thirsty one rebuked him. "Don't you fear God since you are under the same sentence? We are punished justly, for we are getting what our deeds deserve. But this man has done nothing wrong" (verses 40–41). Later Jesus would say to the thirsty one, "Today you will be with me in paradise" (verse 43).

Even at His death, Jesus confounded the world. The people of His day didn't know what to do with Him. He spoke in riddles, healed the sick, and raised the dead. Jesus bewildered the people of His day. He confounds people now.

And the reason we are so confounded is that we always want to make Jesus into someone He isn't. I'd like to suggest three things Jesus isn't. And three things Jesus is. I know this list could be never-ending, but I want to focus on three misconceptions about Jesus that relate to how He confounds the world and how His identity becomes utterly arresting and transforming.

You are taking Jesus into the world. It will be helpful to understand how He confounds it.

Not Nice, but Astonishing

When asked to describe Jesus, most people, even many Christians, would say He was a nice man. Perhaps what they mean is that He was kind. Or perhaps they mean He was good. Probably they have pictures from Bible storybooks in their heads and imagine Jesus sitting down with lambs and think of Him as gentle. Some might mean Jesus was pleasant and a great guy to hang out with.

I don't think those descriptions are necessarily wrong, but they sure miss the point. And in many ways they're misleading. Sort of like saying Peyton Manning was an okay quarterback.

Author Tim Hansel has said that Jesus was "shocking, astonishing,... daring, revolutionary,...but *nice*?" No. It would surprise many to know that the Bible never describes Him as nice.[1]

That doesn't mean Jesus *wasn't* nice, but nothing about that word captures the essence of who Jesus was. Or is.

For those who encountered Jesus on earth, those who entered the presence of God in the flesh, it was like stepping into the path of a hurricane. It was dangerous. It was risky. And it was always life changing. If we imagine those people who crossed Jesus's path two thousand years ago as having pleasant smiles on their faces, we've got it all wrong. More likely they were walking around with their jaws hanging open.

Jesus was astonishing. No one had ever encountered anyone like Him before. This hurricane left in His wake people shaking their heads, doing double takes, and saying, "You've got to be kidding me!" This astonishing man had people running home breathless to tell family and friends, "You're not gonna believe this!"

And this mysterious person dared to defy the powerful religious leaders of His day, leaving them screaming at Him, "Don't you dare talk to us like that!"

They considered Him a heretic, a usurper, a rabble-rouser, an evil spirit, a demon.

No one seemed to find reason to describe Jesus as nice.

Now, if you read closely, you'll find in the Bible the same divided world we've been talking about: the skeptics and the thirsty.

In John 10, Jesus is talking to a crowd about who He is. He talks about sheep and a gate and wolves coming to harm the sheep. At one point He describes Himself as the gate for the sheep; a moment later He identifies Himself as the shepherd (verse 11). He talks about laying down His life for His sheep and then refers to His "authority to take it up again" (verse 18).

Scripture then says, "The Jews who heard these words were again divided. Many of them said, 'He is demon-possessed and raving mad. Why listen to him?'" (verses 19–20). Sounds like skeptic talk to me.

And then, "Others said, 'These are not the sayings of a man possessed by a demon. Can a demon open the eyes of the blind?'" (verse 21). Can't you just hear their thirsty voices?

Neither skeptics nor the thirsty were anywhere close to calling Jesus nice. Either He was a raving lunatic, or He was a miracle worker. Either way He was utterly, jaw-droppingly, amazingly astonishing. Seeing Him in person, you might have thought you were watching a train wreck happening, or you might have believed He was a thunderstorm bringing much-needed rain to sweep out the mess and provide quenching water.

But you wouldn't have thought He was just a nice guy.

However, I do think there's an example in Scripture of someone who might have thought Jesus was nice, one who considered Him perfectly harmless.

Pontius Pilate was the Roman governor who presided over Jesus's trial. As the Roman in charge, he had authority over Jerusalem, a town made up predominantly of Jews. Even so, he had a riot on his hands. The Jewish leaders had incited the populace against Jesus, but Pilate, after questioning Jesus and looking at the charges, said, "I find no basis for a charge against this man." Later he repeated, "He has done nothing to deserve death." And later he again said, "I have found in him no grounds for the death penalty" (Luke 23:4, 15, 22).

Of course, ultimately the Jews clamored for Jesus's death and got what they wanted. Pilate eventually said the equivalent of "Whatever!" and gave Jesus over to them to be crucified.

Now, I don't know about you, but I've always had a soft spot for Pilate. Here's a guy, a Roman, not a believer, but it seems he was trying to save Jesus. I've always thought that Pilate was sort of a good guy.

But in reading this more closely, I see a different angle. The Jews were demanding Jesus's execution because He was claiming to be the Messiah, the King of the Jews. They thought He was a liar, a fraud.

Pilate, on the other hand, looked at Jesus as harmless. Maybe a little loony, but not guilty. Benign. Pilate saw Jesus as a nice man who just got into a bad situation, someone *who really didn't matter*.

In the person of Pontius Pilate, we have a symbol of many people today. When people say that Jesus is nice, it's really a way for them to be a Pilate, a way for them to be dismissive. "Oh, he's fine, he's harmless. Believe if you want. Or not. Whatever." What they're really saying is that Jesus doesn't matter.

And I think that's one of the biggest surprises you and I face as we take our life message into the world. Our toughest challenge usually won't come from those who are passionately against Him. Our biggest challenge comes from those who think Jesus is really just a nice guy.

The real Jesus demands to be considered as more than nice or harmless or benign. He is astonishing in every way, two thousand years ago as well as today. One can argue that Jesus was a liar (as the Jewish leaders did back then) or that He was who He said He was. But you can't argue that He was irrelevant. On earth Jesus performed bewildering miracles, among them turning water into wine, making a blind man see, casting out demons, and raising a man from the dead.

And you know, today *you* are His miracle.

My heart resonates with the lyrics of the David Crowder song "How He Loves." The song says that Jesus "loves like a hurricane." He truly is a hurricane who rips through our lives and turns them upside down, transforming our world.

This is not the work of a nice man.

This is the work of an astonishing God.

Not Legalistic, but Freeing

If you read the Bible honestly, you can't fill in the blank about who Jesus is with the word *legalistic.* Or the word *judgmental.* Or the word *religious.*

Yet all three of those words are part of the picture that the world has of Jesus. Ask someone on the street who Jesus is, and they'll likely say He was the founder of a religion. Or they'll talk about His being a moral person who set a standard we need to live up to. Or they'll jump past the question and start talking about Christians who are judgmental.

I'm aware that a lot of these reactions are based on people's early life experiences with the church. Too many were hurt by a legalistic upbringing, often fueled by a church that was judgmental. Too many have been turned off by religion that's been an empty practice of rules and regulations. I'm afraid that people often transfer negative experiences like these onto the person of Jesus.

It breaks my heart. It's certainly not the Jesus I've come to know. And it's not the Jesus of the Bible.

In John 9 the story is told of Jesus healing a blind man. The man had been blind from birth. Jesus knelt down and formed some clay out of dirt. He applied the clay to the man's eyes and then told the man to wash the clay from his eyes in the pool of Siloam. The man did so and came back with his sight restored.

Not long after, the Pharisees—the legalistic, judgmental religious leaders of that time—spoke to the man who'd been blind. They learned that Jesus had healed this man on the Sabbath, a transgression of the rules and regulations they held so dear. They accused Jesus of sinning because He had violated the rules of the holy day.

This stuns me. *Really?!* Jesus has healed a man—brought back his eyesight!—and the Pharisees couldn't focus on anything but the fact that it happened on the Sabbath. Their legalism got in the way of seeing Jesus for who He was. They were the ones who were truly blind! "Some of the Pharisees said, 'This man is not from God, for he does not keep the Sabbath.' But others asked, 'How can a sinner perform such signs?'" (verse 16).

Skeptics and the thirsty.

Another interesting piece of the story is what Jesus's disciples asked before the blind man was healed. They wondered whether it was the man's sin or his parents' sin that had caused his blindness. Their assumption was one of judgment; this bad thing had happened as punishment and must have been the result of sin. Even Jesus's disciples were prone to view the world in terms of sin and judgment.

Isn't that so like a lot of people today? Isn't that so like, unfortunately, many of us Christians? No wonder the world thinks that the church and Christianity and Jesus Himself are all about legalism and judgment.

Jesus's response to His disciples was completely contrary to what they expected. "'Neither this man nor his parents sinned,' said Jesus, 'but this happened so that the works of God might be displayed in him'" (verse 3). In a single sentence, Jesus overturned the tables of religious legalism, disarming the skeptics and offering freedom to the thirsty.

This is not an isolated story. The Gospels report numerous accounts of Jesus's run-ins with the religious leadership of the day. Jesus healed a paralyzed man and told him his sins were forgiven. The Pharisees challenged Him, accusing Him of blasphemy (Matthew 9:1–3). Jesus found Matthew, a tax collector, and called him to become one of His disciples, so the Pharisees accused Him of associating with "tax collectors and sinners" (verses 10–11). Jesus was challenged on why He and His disciples did not observe the religious rules about fasting. He responded, "How can the guests of the bridegroom mourn while he is with them? The time will come when the bridegroom will be taken from them; then they will fast" (verse 15). He was referring to Himself, of course. He was saying His accusers *were observing religion while missing the point of their faith*—Jesus Himself.

Time and time and time again Jesus stood against legalism, deplored the judgmentalism of the skeptics, and offered a flood of refreshing water to the thirsty.

He is utterly confounding.

And utterly freeing.

NOT DISTANT, BUT PURSUING

Recently I was watching a YouTube video of street interviews in which people were asked who they thought Jesus was. I was encouraged that at least some said they believed He was the Son of God. One young woman said that Jesus was alive today and lived in her heart.

Beautiful!

But I was also struck by the number of people who described Jesus as an old white man with a beard who lived far away in heaven. The gist of these comments was that Jesus was distant, removed, disconnected from the world and from them. As theologian John Stott has written, "Many people visualize a God who sits comfortably on a distant throne, remote, aloof, uninterested and indifferent to the needs of mortals, until, it may be, they can badger him into taking action on their behalf."[2]

I shake my head at this all-too-common view of God but then suddenly feel a gut check. Have we as Christians conveyed, perhaps unwittingly, that God is far off? Have we told people in one way or another that God is not "with you" but is housed somewhere deep inside a church? Have we communicated to people that they need to come to church because God is there and only there?

John Stott continues to reflect on this prevalent idea: "Such a view is wholly false. The Bible reveals a God who, long before it even occurs to us to turn to him, while we are still lost in darkness and sunk in sin, takes the initiative, rises from his throne, lays aside his glory, and stoops to seek until he finds him."[3]

The story of God is precisely the opposite of what the world thinks. God is not far off on a throne somewhere. He does not ask us to search the world high and low to find Him. He does not require us to measure up to become close to Him. God is not hidden somewhere. He is not aloof and distant and apart. God did not wait for us to make the first move. Not at all.

The truth is, *God* is pursing *us*. Relentlessly. He is chasing us.

How do we know this?

Jesus.

Jesus embodies God's pursuit of us. God entered into our mess through Jesus and became human like us so He could draw us to Himself. If God had remained aloof, there would be no Jesus walking among us on earth. Jesus is God-made-human for the purpose of pursuing us. Jesus is the physical evidence of God's passionate desire to be with us and bring us back to Him.

As Howard Macy said, "While we have been pursuing God he has been rushing toward us with reckless love, arms flung wide to hug us home."[4]

Philip Yancey told a personal story of his realization of God's pursuit of him:

I remember a long night sitting in uncomfortable Naugahyde chairs in O'Hare Airport, waiting impatiently for a flight that was delayed for five hours. I happened to be next to a wise woman who was traveling to the same conference. The long delay and the late hour combined to create a melancholy mood.... I was writing the book *Disappointment with God* at the time, and I felt burdened by other people's pains and sorrows, doubts and unanswered prayers.

My companion listened to me in silence for a very long time, and then out of nowhere she asked a question that has always stayed with me. "Philip, do you ever just let God love you?" she said. "It's pretty important, I think."

I realized with a start that she had brought to light a gaping hole in my spiritual life. For all my absorption in the Christian faith, I had missed the most important message of all. The story of Jesus is the story of a celebration, a story of love. It involves pain and disappointment, yes, for God as well as for us. But Jesus embodies the promise of a God who will go any length to win us back.[5]

God wants His family back.

Jesus explained it this way. He was speaking to a crowd and told them a story about a shepherd with a hundred sheep. One goes missing. Jesus puts it rhetorically to those listening: "Doesn't [the shepherd] leave the ninety-nine in the open country and go after the lost sheep until he finds it? And when he finds it, he joyfully puts it on his shoulders and goes home. Then he calls his friends and neighbors together and says, 'Rejoice with me; I have found my lost sheep.' I tell you that in the same way there will be more rejoicing in heaven over one sinner who repents than over ninety-nine righteous persons who do not need to repent" (Luke 15:4–7).

The picture painted here is one of a God who pursues, a God who rejoices when He finds the one who was lost, a God who celebrates getting His child back.

This is a message that the world doesn't understand. It is the dimension of Christianity that makes it radically different from other religions—God is personally, deeply, relentlessly involved in our lives. Maybe because other religions have views of a god or gods that are aloof and cold and distant, the world has the misconception that likewise Jesus is an aloof old man with a white beard.

But maybe that misconception is out there because they have never seen a God who is personally involved or a person who recklessly loves them as Jesus does.

As the hands and feet of Jesus, we are called to join God in His pursuit.

You and I become part of the search-and-rescue team for lost sheep—all of them, including the skeptical and the thirsty.

THE POWER OF JESUS IN YOU

The greatest power of the gospel is the simple presence of Jesus. The world sees Jesus in you. You can be the gospel to them.

Your life, your life message, will illuminate for others a Jesus who is not benign like a "nice guy" but astonishing like a hurricane.

Your life, your life message, will represent to others a Jesus who is not judgmental but freeing and freedom giving.

Your life, your life message, will show others a Jesus who is not aloof and distant but is actively and passionately pursuing them.

I think we try too hard. If we are willing to simply *be* the gospel to the world, it will see Jesus in us.

Our life message should make unbelievers question their disbelief in God.

He will take care of the rest.

The Divine Whisper

1. Pray and ask Jesus to shine through your life today.

2. Read 2 Corinthians 4:5–7 and meditate on the truth that the treasure of Jesus Christ lives in you: "For what we preach is not ourselves, but Jesus Christ as Lord, and ourselves as your servants for Jesus' sake. For God, who said, 'Let light shine out of darkness,' made his light shine in our hearts to give us the light of the knowledge of God's glory displayed in the face of Christ. But we have this treasure in jars of clay to show that this all-surpassing power is from God and not from us."

3. Spend five minutes in silence just letting God love you.

Love the One in Front of You

1. Thank God that you are an ordinary jar of clay but that the treasure of His power shines through you.

2. Ask God to open your eyes to the brokenhearted today. Don't try to solve their problems. Just "be Jesus" to them. Let the love of Christ shine through you.

Part 4

Taking...

Your Life Message to the World Around You

our life is a unique message to the world. You are the gospel, carrying the life of Jesus Christ inside you. That gospel is a powerful message the world has no explanation for. And now God is calling you to take this life message on the road. To put it into action. To actually be the hands and feet of Jesus in the world.

When we understand our lives and the gospel in this revolutionary way and catch the vision that we are to be the message, God's calling suddenly feels fresh, new.

The words of Christ before He ascended into heaven may be very familiar to you: "You will receive power when the Holy Spirit comes on you; and you will be my witnesses in Jerusalem, and in all Judea and Samaria, and to the ends of the earth" (Acts 1:8). But now we understand more clearly that the message is not about empty words and endless sermons. It means being witnesses to the reality of Christ on earth and to His transformation of our lives.

The last part of that verse is interesting: "and you will be my witnesses in Jerusalem, and in all Judea and Samaria, and to the ends of the earth." Jerusalem, Judea, Samaria, and the ends of the earth. What does that mean for you and me today?

Well, we might consider those four areas as four concentric circles around us right now: our town, our state, our region, the world itself. Jesus was saying that we are to be ripples in a pond, that being the message starts by making waves right where we are, then farther out, and then farther out still.

At the dawn of the first century, Jerusalem was the center of the Jewish world. Until AD 70 it was the site of the temple, the location of the Most Holy Place, and the only location where sacrifices could be properly offered. It also was the place where the disciples were located when the Spirit came at Pentecost. When Jesus said, "You will be my witnesses in Jerusalem," He was saying, "Start here," and that's what they did. Peter walked out of the upper room where they'd been praying when the Spirit fell, and he started preaching right there in front of the house (see Acts 2).

For you and me also, this is where it makes sense to begin. At home. In our communities. In our local towns. We can't skip over our families and neighborhoods to reach the world.

So what does being the message look like for you right now, right where you are?

Be careful not to overthink this. The most important first steps are usually the most obvious; they're the simple, direct actions that we've often overlooked or avoided. God isn't asking you to save the world. He can handle that Himself. He needs you to be the message right where you are.

So what can you do to make a difference locally? Take a few moments right now to think about it. Doing something new, something outside of your personal space, is a key step in being the message. You see, it doesn't just involve lending a hand, doing needed work, or volunteering. Those are all good things, but being the message isn't limited to your physical labor in helping and doing good. It means putting yourself out there in your local community so that your life message can be seen.

The point is to get started. *You can do more than nothing.*

Take a moment to consider the people near you. Not only your family but friends. Not only friends but neighbors. Not only neighbors but the needy family or homeless person or struggling teenager a mile away. Pray about it. Whom is God calling you to reach out to? What name is He whispering to you?

It's not about how many people you can reach. It's about reaching out to someone. *Love the one in front of you.*

Being the message transforms everything. This isn't about missions and missionaries, as we've been taught for ages. It's about our lives being real and authentic, uniquely reflecting the message of Jesus to people who cross our paths every day.

You see, there is someone in your world who has a you-size need inside.

God is calling you to be the gospel to that person.

God doesn't ask us to do
something big for Him.
He asks us to take small
steps of faith so He can do
something big in us.

10

More Than Nothing

We cannot do everything at once, but we can do something at once.

Calvin Coolidge

Even the largest avalanche is triggered by small things.

Vernor Vinge

F our and a half million tourists visit the Grand Canyon every year. Most get no farther than the railing along the rim, where they stand and gaze into the immense beauty of the canyon. They look, just as if they were home watching TV and a National Geographic special on the Grand Canyon was on.

Harvey Butchart was thirty-eight the first time he stood at the rim of the canyon. Unlike the hundreds who stood with him that day, Butchart wasn't content merely to look at the Grand Canyon; he wanted to experience it. So he stepped onto a path and made his way down the canyon wall toward the Colorado River.

Hours later, Harvey knelt at the bank of the Colorado, put his hand in the river, and felt the cool water wash over his skin. That experience changed his life.

Butchart would return again and again to hike the canyon, traveling from end to end, logging some twelve thousand miles in the process. He was the first person to hike the entire length of the canyon. During his life he discovered 108 approaches to the Colorado River and scaled the canyon wall in 164 places. When he died at the age of ninety-five, he was hailed as the greatest Grand Canyon expert who ever lived.[1]

Harvey Butchart wasn't content to look at the Grand Canyon. He needed to touch it.

The First Step

We are called to be the message, live the gospel, and then take our life message on the road. But taking that first step is one of the hardest things we will ever do.

Unlike Harvey Butchart, many of us would rather watch life than touch it. We'd often prefer to give our money to a need rather than give ourselves to it. I know that at times I've talked myself out of doing something and talked myself into sitting back and watching.

Why?

As I gaze out at the problems of the world, even just the world around me, the task ahead appears vast and overwhelming. I'm just one person. How can I possibly make a difference? The need is so massive. Unfortunately when I get into this place—I call it the Valley of the Overwhelmed—I too often talk myself out of taking my life message from words to actions.

There's a little chat I have with myself, and it goes like this: *I'm not ready to help someone else in need. My own life is still too much of a mess. I need to get myself together first.*

Well, God doesn't ask us to solve all the world's problems. He doesn't ask us to wait until we have our lives together. If we wait for the means to correct every ill of society or for all our own problems to get resolved, we'll spend our whole lives waiting.

Truth is, I don't need to have my life together, and I'm not "just one person." God's on my side. And maybe you've noticed: He's a difference maker.

There's a breathtaking account in the Old Testament of a miracle God performed. Three enemy nations formed a coalition to attack God's people in Judah. As the coalition army entered the valley for battle, the people of Judah, led by King Jehoshaphat, felt outnumbered and doomed to failure (see 2 Chronicles 20:1–4). In that moment the valley of plenty they'd known for so long became their version of the Valley of the Overwhelmed.

For you and me, the enemies aren't physical armies pushing toward us but the armies of anxiety, depression, and worry marching across the horizon of our lives. Money. Jobs. Children. Regrets from the past. Old habits we've struggled to overcome that return with a vengeance. And on top of it all, the sense of our smallness and weakness in the face of overwhelming need. These are the forces the Enemy uses to keep us from being the message to the world around us.

Jehoshaphat, faced with the very real possibility that his kingdom would be destroyed, prayed a simple prayer: "We do not know what to do, but our eyes are on you" (verse 12). What a perfect prayer to remember the next time you need to get out of the Valley of the Overwhelmed!

God heard Jehoshaphat's prayer and gave His answer through Jahaziel, a man who was standing nearby while the king prayed. Jahaziel said, "This is what the LORD says to you: 'Do not be afraid or discouraged because of this vast army. For the battle is not yours, but God's. Tomorrow march down against them. They will be climbing up by the Pass of Ziz, and you will find them at the end of the gorge in the Desert of Jeruel. You will not have to fight this battle. Take up your positions; stand firm and see the deliverance the LORD will give you, Judah and Jerusalem. Do not be afraid; do not be discouraged. Go out to face them tomorrow, and the LORD will be with you'" (verses 15–17).

Here's the part I really love: *"You will not have to fight this battle."*

When we struggle to take that first step, when we feel overwhelmed by the enormity of the task and our seeming insignificance, when we are so focused on our own problems and weaknesses, God says to us, "Relax. You don't have to fight this battle. I've got this. And oh, by the way, some folks over here need your help."

The Bible goes on to tell us that God planned ambushes for the coalition enemy armies. They surprised one another, fought one another—and destroyed one another. When Jehoshaphat's army entered town, the battle was already over. Just as God had said (see verses 22–23).

Often the miracle we need most is for God to open our spiritual eyes so we can see the reality of who He is and what He can do. We are never outnumbered by our obstacles. The One who created the universe is with us in every situation we face.

"You will not have to fight this battle."

That changes everything.

THE ADVENTURE OF A LIFETIME

If you're paying attention, you'll be asking some questions right now: Why did God go to the trouble of giving the army of Judah such specific instructions? Why did He even have them show up on the battlefield if, in fact, He was going to destroy the enemy armies anyway?

And, by the way, why does God enlist me to be the message in the world near and far? He can help people if He wants to. He can work miracles to save people from anything and everything. After all, He's pretty capable of handling things on His own.

Good question.

One key part of the answer is that God wants us to have the joy and adventure of participating in the work and the miracles He's doing in the world. He doesn't want us to watch Him on TV. He wants us to touch other people's needs and experience His remarkable power and provision in their lives.

We should all be Harvey Butchart. Rather than being content to watch while God works in the lives of others, we should take His hand and allow Him to lead us on a journey: An adventure to scale the walls and hike the trails of His calling. An adventure to put our hands in the river of God's mysteries. An adventure to sense His power at work in our lives in dramatic and poignant ways.

Too many times we hang back where it's safe instead of stepping out on a journey of faith, trusting God completely. He wants us to have a life of adventure, risking much to gain much, risking all to gain all.

Yet risk is something you and I usually work hard to avoid. Even when we do catch a glimpse of the kind of adventurous life we were meant to live, we shrink back and cower in fear at the risk that kind of life involves. That's unfortunate, because we're the ones missing out.

Our deliverance from the Valley of the Overwhelmed is just around the corner, and we'll reach it by taking the first step toward the God of Overcoming.

When Harvey Butchart set out to explore the Grand Canyon, he didn't climb over the railing in the visitor area and jump. He took a trail that led to the bottom. Doing that required only one thing: for him to take the first step, followed by another, then another.

While there are all kinds of reasons you might talk yourself out of taking that first step, accepting God's invitation to adventure and putting your life message into a life of action, there's one irrefutable fact you simply cannot argue away: *you can do more than nothing.*

Any little something helps. And God can take that little something and multiply the effects far more than you could ever imagine. He uses your small part to make a giant difference in the lives of others.

Yes, you're just one person. But the fact is you can do more than nothing.

THE POWER OF ONE LIFE

Several years ago we took a small step into the Kware Slum outside Nairobi, Kenya, and it became a God adventure that has changed our lives.

We began working with a group of Kenyan young people who were being the message of Christ in their own neighborhood. One of the leaders of the group is a young man named Oscar. We met him during our first visit to Kenya, and now he's one of our full-time pastors there.

Oscar grew up in the slums and spends a lot of time in the dusty, chaotic schools, building relationships with the students and encouraging teachers. When we bring our young people from Woodlands Church, they work side by side with kids from the neighborhood to share the gospel with the students through music and skits.

On a recent trip we went with Oscar and the team to five or six schools in the slums. On the last day we visited an elementary school. After the presentation many of the children crowded around us, insisting we talk to them. They squeezed our hands tight and didn't want to let go. All the while they said things like "Don't forget me" and "Take me back to America."

Feelings of hopelessness overwhelmed me as I knew it was time for us to go and they would be staying in that painful and desperate slum. I began to wonder if anything we were doing made a difference. Exhausted and discouraged, I climbed into the van to leave and saw Oscar seated next to me. Seeing him there reminded me of how God changes things one life at a time.

When Oscar was a young boy, he was a student at that very same school we'd just visited. As he grew older, he began using drugs and became a bad influence on other students, leading many of them into lives of drug abuse and addiction. He was warned several times to change his conduct, but he refused and eventually was kicked out of school. Still, he didn't change, and at the age of eighteen, his parents kicked him out of the house.

Left with no place to go, he went to the nearest church and prayed a desperate prayer: "God, if You save me from this mess, I'm going to serve You all my life." Oscar gave his life to Christ that day and began attending church. The youth group encouraged him in his new walk with God. Now, eight years later, Oscar was leading the group. He had gone from being a message of despair to being a message of hope in the slum where he grew up.

Our trips to the schools a few times each year may not make a big difference by themselves, but we can multiply that effort by encouraging and supporting Oscar and the team in Nairobi as they visit the schools every week. They connect with students, parents, teachers, and administrators regularly, and those ongoing relationships have an effect far greater than anything we could do on our own.

The greatest miracle of all is a changed life. The problem is that sometimes we become so overwhelmed by the number of lives that are hurting, we forget the power of one life to change the world.

One of our church ministries recently took us to Sweden, where we participated in a pastors' conference and spoke at several churches. We arrived in Sweden a few days early because I (Chris) wanted to see the small town where my great-grandfather Sven Nelson grew up. As a child, I'd heard about him through family stories but never knew where he grew up. Dear Swedish friends met us at the airport, and with their help we found the tiny village of Ynde and even saw the church where he was confirmed at the age of fourteen.

After a few minutes the experience welled up inside me. In a burst of excitement, I climbed atop a big rock and yelled, "Sven, I'm home!" More than nostalgia or the affirmation of finding my roots, as I stood there in that village, I became keenly aware of the seemingly causal connection that linked my present life with that of my great-grandfather, a man I never even knew.

At the age of twenty-two, Sven made the choice to leave that little village for the first time and travel across the ocean to America in the hope of a better life. It was the adventure of a lifetime. Of several lifetimes. By taking that step, he was engaging in an adventure that would radically affect not only his life but others' as well, including mine. The decision he made back then put me where I am today.

The choices you make today will affect many people for years to come.

Our decisions, good and bad, will keep on affecting people like ripples in a pond. It's inescapable. And if you're considering not making a decision because you're fearful of making the wrong one, there's something else you need to know. Choosing not to make a decision is a decision in itself. No matter what you do, your life message will ripple through the ages.

CHRIST AND CAFFEINE

Following the Haitian earthquake in 2010, our work there became a long-term project. We returned again and again with teams of volunteers who brought medical supplies, water-purification equipment, and food.

It sounds like we knew what we were doing. We didn't. But we'd taken a first step. Then another. Then another... Step by step we expanded from that first feeble attempt in an effort to bring lasting and sustainable change to the lives of the Haitians with whom we worked.

On one of our trips, some friends said, "All the aid and relief groups stay in Port-au-Prince, but almost no one ministers to the people in the mountains." So we went up there to an area known as Marmelade to see what conditions were like and to find out whether we could help.

The area was isolated and very poor, but they had an abundance of beautiful, raw, unroasted coffee beans. However, due to the remote location and poor roads, coffee buyers rarely came through that area, and consequently most of the coffee-bean crop went unharvested. When we arrived, much of it lay on the ground.

Seeing that, we decided to make a difference in the Marmelade region, not by giving them buildings and supplies, but by buying their coffee. We made a great team: they were good at growing coffee, and we were good at drinking it! That first year we purchased their entire crop, about ten thousand pounds. We imported it to the United States, trucked it to a roaster in Houston, and recruited volunteers from the church, who packaged it for sale. We use it at the church and sell it in our coffee shop and bookstore.

The next logical step was to recruit a coffee expert, who traveled to the region and trained the farmers in better growing techniques. With his help the farmers tripled their production to thirty thousand pounds. The year after that they harvested seventy thousand pounds. With the money they earn from coffee sales, the people of Marmelade are able to build the things they need: homes, churches, schools, and a community center. We're there helping them, and as a result we have unique opportunities to share the gospel in far more meaningful ways than if we used words alone.

This was an effort of a whole church to be the message. But the process for you and me as individuals is the same: begin with who you are, address the needs you find, and go deep with the intention of making lasting, self-sustaining change. See a need; fill a need.

That's what it means to be the message. That's what happens when you step out in faith. God opens doors. When you refuse to close your eyes to the plight of the poor and the powerless, God works. When you enter into the adventure God has for you, He works miracles.

I have a friend named Harrell who is an accomplished businessman, but in his spare time he loves to coach and umpire Little League baseball games. He grew up playing the great American pastime and even played in college.

When Harrell discovered that a Native American reservation our church had been working with in New Mexico needed a baseball diamond, he volunteered to help. Harrell and nine other baseball enthusiasts went to the reservation and spent their hard-earned vacation time to help the locals build the field, backstop, and dugouts.

It's true: if you build it, they will come! Now the reservation has a youth baseball league that makes a huge impact in the community.

What I love most is that Harrell and his buddies weren't pastors or full-time missionaries. They were just guys who loved Jesus, enjoyed baseball, and cared about kids. Until that trip they had no idea God would use their interest in baseball as a tool to be the message to so many young people.

Remember, all you have to do is take a step of obedience, and God does the rest. It doesn't require much.

Just you.

Just the power of your life message.

ONE LIFE DECLARATION

Several years ago we wrote a declaration to the Lord acknowledging the power of one life placed in His hands and committing our lives to His purpose. We call it our "One Life Declaration," and it helps us remember that God changes the world one life at a time. Every life matters to God.

Our declaration says:

I believe with all my heart that two thousand years ago the sacrifice of one life, Jesus Christ, changed my one life for all eternity.

I believe Christ gave His life for every life; therefore, it is impossible to measure the value of one life.

So I declare that as long as there is one life that has never experienced the love of Christ, as long as there is…

- one child without clean water
- one mother afflicted with AIDS
- one family with no shelter
- one man who is homeless and hungry
- one teenager who feels hopeless
- one person who has never head the gospel

I will do whatever it takes, with whatever I have, with my one and only life to help one more person experience Christ's love.

I refuse to live in a selfish bubble in my own little world by closing my eyes to the hurting and hopeless all around me.

I refuse to come to the end of my life and realize I missed my one and only chance with my one and only life to give my all to the One who gave His life for me.

That's our declaration, and with God's power we intend to fulfill it. We're ordinary, imperfect people, but we serve an extraordinary God who wants to do extraordinary things through us.

We challenge you. Make a commitment between you and the Lord to allow Him to use your one and only life.

You can do more than nothing.

Just take the first step.

The Divine Whisper

1. Read 2 Chronicles 20:15–17: "This is what the LORD says: Do not be afraid! Don't be discouraged by this mighty army, for the battle is not yours, but God's. Tomorrow, march out against them. You will find them coming up through the ascent of Ziz at the end of the valley that opens into the wilderness of Jeruel. But you will not even need to fight. Take your positions; then stand still and watch the LORD's victory. He is with you, O people of Judah and Jerusalem. Do not be afraid or discouraged. Go out against them tomorrow, for the LORD is with you!" (NLT).

2. What is the battle you're facing?

3. Spend five minutes in silence remembering that God is with you, restoring your soul and fighting for you.

Love the One in Front of You

1. Write out your own One Life Declaration, and ask God to give you the faith to take the next step in your journey to be the message.

2. Pray about getting involved in your church's mission efforts, either locally or abroad, believing God will guide you and provide the path.

You can't change the world
by stepping over the
people closest to you.

#BeTheMessage

11

Love the One in Front of You

True compassion means not only feeling another's pain but also being moved to help relieve it.
    Daniel Goleman

Love begins by taking care of the closest ones—the ones at home.

    Mother Teresa

I f you're like me, you have a desire to make a difference in the world, but you struggle with finding the right opportunity. When a big opportunity comes around, you're busy; life has preoccupied you. Then when you do have time, the opportunities don't seem to show up. And just as we do in so many other areas, we make this more complicated than it needs to be.

It's easy to unintentionally compartmentalize our life message. We have our family life, our work life, our church life, and our recreation-and-hobbies life. Being the message is relegated to a little corner, say, every few months on a Saturday at a soup kitchen. Or mailing a monthly check to a humanitarian organization. Or contributing to someone else's mission trip.

Those are all good things to do, but that way of thinking is limited and incomplete. You can't mail in your life message. You have to live it.

What I'm learning is that I have it all wrong.

Being the message is not about someday, over there, sometime. It's about now, here, and always.

EVERYONE HAS A STORY

In conjunction with the youth group at our church, I (Chris) had agreed to host a large group of students at our house.

As it turned out, on the day of the event, everything went horribly wrong at home. The washing machine overflowed and flooded the laundry-room floor. While I was busy cleaning up the mess, our dogs got loose and bolted down the street. After corralling them, I sat down at my desk to sort through correspondence, and my computer crashed. The washer repairman never showed up, and by then the day was all but gone.

It was then that I remembered the students were coming to the house that night, and I had nothing to feed them. I hurried to the grocery store. It was raining when I arrived, and all the parking spaces near the door were taken. I had no umbrella, so I made a mad dash through the rain to the front door of the store. You can imagine my state of mind as I sloshed through the store—sopping wet, cold, and pressed for time.

I grabbed a few bags of chips and a couple of bottles of soda, counting the items to stay under the ten-item limit for the express-checkout lane, and hurried to the front of the store. The nearest express lane had only one customer, so I pushed my cart over to it and began unloading.

That's when I discovered the woman ahead of me had far more than ten items. Not only that, but she moved at a maddeningly slow pace, setting each item on the counter one by one, as if in a daze. I watched and waited, my items already in place, as the tension inside began to rise.

The students would arrive at the house in just a few minutes. I had to get through the checkout line and out of that store.

Finally the woman set her last item on the counter. I watched in nervous anguish as she rummaged through her purse, searching for her bank card. She couldn't find it. Time was ticking away. The students. My house. What was this woman doing?

She checked the pockets inside the purse, then ran her hand deeper to check along the bottom. Finally she turned the purse upside down and emptied the contents onto the counter.

By then I was steaming. The cashier was too, along with the people in line behind me. They sighed and huffed with indignation at the thoughtlessness of this bumbling woman who was holding up the line. Inwardly I fumed, *It's called the "express lane" for a reason, lady.* Maybe she didn't have any reason to be in a hurry, but the rest of us sure did.

Just then she glanced awkwardly up at me. In an apologetic voice she said, "I'm so sorry. I'm not usually like this. I've been at the hospital all day and just brought my daughter home from her first chemo treatment. I wanted to get her some groceries, things she might be able to keep down. I was trying to hurry back home to her. I'm really sorry for making you wait."

I was devastated. This woman was carrying a load far heavier than any I had ever known. Yet all it took for me to judge her was a few minutes of inconvenience and a handful of items in a grocery cart.

I reached past her and handed the cashier my bank card. "Just add her things to mine," I said.

The woman looked at me with a grateful smile. "Thank you," she said.

I mumbled in response, "No problem." I'm sure it looked like a gallant gesture, me using my bank card to purchase groceries for a stranger, but truthfully it was an act of repentance. I felt so ashamed of the judgmental thoughts I'd entertained about her.

When I finished at the checkout, I slowly walked back to my car, no longer aware of the rain or the time. Seated behind the steering wheel, I dropped my head and wept. I cried for the daughter who was hurting, for the mother trying to hurry home, and for me as I considered the ungrateful, self-centered person I'd become.

Since that day things have changed for me. Now when I encounter frustrating drivers, annoying customer-service representatives, and slow shoppers, I realize that we never really know anyone else's reality. The person we're tempted to judge might be living a nightmare. I've learned that the person who annoys me might need me the most.

I've learned that being the message means loving the person right in front of me.

EXPECTING THE UNEXPECTED

Who is the one right in front of you?

The events surrounding Jesus's birth are familiar to us all. Caesar Augustus ordered a census of the Roman world. People had to register in their ancestral hometowns. For Joseph, that meant traveling with a very pregnant Mary from Nazareth to Bethlehem, some seventy miles away.

While they were in Bethlehem, Mary gave birth.

The Bible describes that event in one short phrase: "She gave birth to her firstborn" (Luke 2:7). I wish the gospel writers had provided more detail. There are things I'd like to know. Did Jesus enter the world wide eyed and quiet or wailing with passion? Did He have a dark mop of curls, or was His head bald and smooth? Details like that are missing from Scripture, but here's something that was noted: Jesus, God in the flesh, had only a manger, a feeding trough, for a cradle "because there was no room for them in the inn" (verse 7, NKJV).

The Greek word for "inn" is *kataluma,* which means "guest house" or "lodging place." This word can be interpreted as a traditional inn or the guest room in a home. Either way, one fact is unavoidable: not one person in the town of Bethlehem gave up his or her room for Jesus. The Creator and Savior of the world was within arm's reach.

And they completely, utterly missed Him.

This story becomes all the more poignant when we place ourselves in it.

If we had been in Bethlehem that day and had seen a pregnant peasant woman pass by on the street, would we have responded any differently? Would we have offered to help ease Mary's discomfort? Would we have given her our room?

No doubt most of us hope we would have reacted differently. We like to think we would have noticed Joseph and Mary and given them a comfortable place to stay, but bring that story forward to today, and you'll get a sense of what the people in Bethlehem encountered. Think of a man and a very pregnant woman stepping off the bus in your city or town. They're tired and grungy from a long trip. You don't know them. They're complete strangers.

Would you help them?

Or would your only response be a muttered prayer of thanks to God that you aren't like them?

WOULD YOU HAVE MISSED JESUS?

I don't know about you, but I can guess what my response would have been. Based on my reaction to the lady in line ahead of me at the grocery store and many similar incidents, I'm sure I would have walked right past them. That's not something I'm comfortable dwelling on, but it's who I am, and it's a part of my character that I have to allow God to refine.

The opportunity the people of Bethlehem had to show kindness to Jesus was no greater than the opportunities you and I have right in front of us every single day. In other words, the real question isn't "Would I have missed Jesus back then?" but *"Did I miss Jesus today?"*

When asked what will happen in the future, Jesus described a scene in which all of us will stand before Him. On that day Jesus will separate us into two groups—those who please Him and those who don't. To those who please Him, He will say, "Take your inheritance, the kingdom prepared for you since the creation of the world. For I was hungry and you gave me something to eat, I was thirsty and you gave me something to drink, I was a stranger and you invited me in, I needed clothes and you clothed me, I was sick and you looked after me, I was in prison and you came to visit me" (Matthew 25:34–36).

Then the ones who please the Lord will ask, "When did we see you hungry and feed you, or thirsty and give you something to drink? When did we see you a stranger and invite you in, or needing clothes and clothe you? When did we see you sick or in prison and go to visit you?"

And Jesus will answer, "Whatever you did for one of the least of these…, you did for me" (verses 37–40).

The way we treat the powerless and the overlooked, not just the people in a foreign land but the ones living next-door, is the message we communicate to the world around us. If we choose to be the message, we're agreeing with God to love the one in front of us, moment by moment, day by day. Actively. Intentionally. Sacrificially.

Is that risky? Absolutely. When we reach out to the people passing us on the sidewalk or standing in line with us at the grocery store, we won't know their stories. We'll have no idea the troubles they're facing or the messes we might invite into our own lives by reaching out to them. But that's what being the message is about—stepping out of our comfort zones and into the messes of the lives around us.

Is a life like that challenging? No question. If you've ever loved a two-year-old throwing a tantrum or a grumpy spouse looking for someone to blame, you have your answer. It's a challenge.

Will it hurt? Without a doubt. There'll be plenty of times when you're overflowing with good feelings, and on those days helping others will come easily. But loving people with the love of Christ means exposing your heart to the pain they're experiencing in their lives. Engaging with other people's pain always hurts.

Will it cost us? Yes. Engaging the world in an active effort to be the gospel in the lives of others will cost money, quite a lot of our time, and nearly all our pride.

Will it be rewarding? Beyond our wildest dreams.

If you're watching for Him, intently waiting to see Him in the routine experiences of life, Jesus will show up in front of you every day, usually disguised as people who are unable to repay even the smallest act of kindness you could show them. Love them anyway. And get ready for the greatest adventure this side of heaven.

Jesus in Disguise

I recently received a letter from Amando and Tammy, a couple who went with us on a missions trip. This was their first missions trip, and they did it as an initial step into the great adventure of loving the one in front of you.

> We never imagined how our lives would be so richly rewarded and
> ultimately changed forever when we decided to take our first missions

trip to the Dominican Republic. Tammy and I thought that trip would be a great way for us to give some of our time to bless and minister the love of Christ to others.

During a particular prayer, as my head was bowed, I noticed a pair of filthy, worn-out, wrong-sized tennis shoes on the feet of a teenage boy. My heart began to ache for that child and every child there, all of whom had similar shoes or no shoes at all. Some kids had one shoe. Some ran barefoot. Those fortunate enough to have shoes at all had them in the worst condition.

On the last day of our trip, the boy whose shoes I had noticed asked me for the shoes on my feet. Initially, I laughed it off. We went about our activities, but as I sat on the bus leaving the site, I realized that I had missed a huge opportunity. Right there on the bus, my desire to help those children in a real way exploded. There was something I had to do.

Amando and Tammy came back to the United States without their tennis shoes but with a dream and a vision from God. They went to work in their local neighborhood, collecting shoes to take to the Dominican Republic. That was only one small step of being the gospel, but it was a step that put shoes on the feet of shoeless children. That was the vision—to give those children shoes—and they worked at it diligently.

But God had something much bigger in mind. Through their effort, The Woodlands Marathon, an annual event held in our area, teamed up with Amando, Tammy, and our church to take that vision to the next level. Together we collected more than ten thousand pairs of shoes to be given to children who had none.

God doesn't ask us to do something big for Him. He just asks us to love the one in front of us. If Amando had ignored the unexpected moment when he looked down and saw the boy's tattered shoes, he would have missed Jesus in disguise and one of the most rewarding experiences of his life. And thousands of children would have missed the blessing of having shoes on their feet.

Keep a sharp eye out for Jesus in disguise today, and love Him where you find Him.

You'll be the one who experiences the miracle.

LIFE MESSAGE MULTIPLIED

Connecting in the body of Christ provides opportunities for you to partner with others to be the message in "Jerusalem, and in all Judea and Samaria, and to the ends of the earth" (Acts 1:8).

Now, this isn't a commercial for church, or for our church specifically, but I want you to understand that being the message isn't always a solo mission. By getting involved with a group, you'll find new possibilities you hadn't even considered.

Our church considers "Jerusalem" to be right here in Houston. God has called us to be the message to the world, but that begins where we are here on the east side of Texas. Our satellite campuses, our work with the poor, our partnering to support homeless missions and to help girls out of sex trafficking in our city—we do all of that because we genuinely believe that our missions outreach effort begins in our own community.

"Judea," to us, is Texas and the wider southeastern region. Actually, Texas is strategically situated between the Southeast and the Southwest, and we send emergency-relief teams in both directions. From the beginning we worked hard to keep our church aware of the needs in our region, but things really took off in response to Hurricane Katrina.

Like you, during Katrina we watched in horror at the plight of thousands of people who were trapped in the New Orleans Superdome. The magnitude of that problem was overwhelming, but when the city of Houston opened the Astrodome to house them, we stepped up to help. By the end of the first day, we were feeding the workers—policemen, firemen, and emergency medical technicians—who kept the massive facility open and operational. We continued to feed them each day as long as the need existed. As a result of that effort, we purchased a forty-foot kitchen trailer and continue to use it in response to disasters and other needs.

A few years later Hurricane Ike hit our area. With trees down everywhere someone suggested we organize crews to help move them out of the way. We put out a call for people with chain saws, and people responded in droves. Nothing like driving around in a pickup and operating a chain saw to ramp up the testosterone level! As the work progressed, we dubbed our crews the "Texas Chain Saw Ministry," and the name stuck. They've been put to good use in the region and continue to work throughout the nation in response to natural disasters. When Hurricane Sandy hit New Jersey and New York, they were among the first to help with cleanup.

"Samaria" for us is something called cross-cultural missions. Samaria was located right next to Judea, but it was a culture unto itself, partly Jewish and partly a conglomeration of other religious ideas. It was so different, in fact, that Jews traveling between Jerusalem and Galilee routinely went around it, adding extra time to their trip in the process, just to avoid the region. In His final words to His disciples, Jesus essentially said, "Not anymore. We're bridging the cultural gap and bringing the good news to the Samaritans." Our country today is as culturally divided as the first-century Middle East. Bring up the topic of immigration in a conversation, and you'll see what I mean. Most of us think of cross-cultural ministry as ministry in a foreign land, but we're engaged in that work right here in the United States.

America is now a multicultural environment. We may still be the melting

pot of old, where cultures are subsumed in another and produce a homoge-
nized lifestyle that reflects the best of all worlds, but the nature of that end
result is changing in dramatic ways. People from some of the most unreached
groups in the world reside right here in American cities.

That's Jerusalem, Judea, and Samaria from our Houston perspective, but
we're also called to the ends of the earth. We're involved in ministry in many
parts of the world, always with an eye to loving the one in front of us.

Your church might offer opportunities for your unique message to reach
the person in front of you. Church might be the engine for your message to
be transported across your state, your region, or the world. It might provide
resources and energy you don't have on your own that can exponentially
change the scope of your circle and multiply your life message.

God calls you to love the one in front of you. He says what you do for
that person is what you do for Him. Regardless of whether we do that on our
own or alongside a church community, our marching orders are clear.

Start right where you are, beginning with the person in front of you.

The Divine Whisper

1. Read Matthew 9:36: "When [Jesus] saw the crowds, he had compassion on them, because they were harassed and helpless, like sheep
   without a shepherd."
2. Really seeing the hurts of the crowd produces compassion. Ask
   Christ to open your eyes to see in your crowded life that one person
   who needs your compassion.
3. Spend five minutes in silence, listening for God's still, small voice
   speaking in your heart.

Love the One in Front of You

1. Watch for Jesus in disguise everywhere you go today.
2. Remember, God doesn't ask you to do something big for Him. He
   asks you to take small steps of obedience to love one person at a
   time. Be intentional. Hunt for hurting people, and ask God to show
   you how you can help.

Your destiny is determined
by where you stand in the
defining moments of life.
#BeTheMessage

Take a Stand

There is a defining moment in every person's life.
Within that moment everything that person is,
shines its brightest.

Anonymous

If you look for truth, you may find comfort in the
end: if you look for comfort you will not get either
comfort or truth—only soft soap and wishful
thinking to begin with and, in the end, despair.

C. S. Lewis

*D*ietrich Bonhoeffer was a man who discovered what it means to live the
message of the gospel.

A young theologian in Germany in the 1920s, Bonhoeffer had studied
God but in a purely academic way. His faith was based on an intellectual
understanding of the Bible and the theological writings of others. Born into
one of Germany's most prestigious families, he had the money, status, and
opportunity to study and teach in the top universities in Germany.

Early in his life Dietrich Bonhoeffer knew about God but really didn't know God personally. For him, at first, the message of the gospel was a set of ideas, not a life lived out. It was religion, not life.

But that would change.

By the early 1930s the German republic was fragile and rapidly changing. The 1929 economic collapse in America had affected the world and was now devastating the German economy, already burdened by the weight of remuneration for World War I. A new, young, angry political philosophy was taking hold: Nazism.

Meanwhile, Dietrich Bonhoeffer traveled to America, a trip that would change his life and his faith. He'd begun to be troubled by the dry intellectualism of his faith and the German church. He knew there had to be something more, but he hadn't found it.

In New York City in 1930, he attended an African American church in Harlem. What Bonhoeffer observed was a vibrancy of worship, a depth of heartfelt faith, and an exuberance of authentic lives living out the truth of Christ. He saw the gospel played out joyfully through people's lives.

It astonished and delighted him. That congregation spoke to his heart, and suddenly he had the experience of faith that had been missing from his life. He'd begun to discover faith not as an intellectual sermon but as a life message. And he discovered something more from that Harlem church—a deep compassion for those who were oppressed. His fellowship with African American Christians brought him face to face with injustice and a new view of the gospel of Jesus Christ, one that rescues those who hurt and are downtrodden.

When he returned to Germany a year later, young Dietrich brought with him a new perspective, his own life message wrapped in the living gospel. Also new in his heart was a keen sensitivity to the plight of the oppressed. And in the political unrest he found upon returning home, Bonhoeffer saw the seeds of oppression.

In 1933, Adolf Hitler was appointed chancellor of the German republic, and he quickly consolidated his power and philosophy in the country. As its grip on life and politics tightened, Nazism began to permeate all of culture, including religion and the church. Savvy enough not to overtly oppose Protestantism in Germany, Hitler cleverly embraced the church, then gradually redefined it in his own terms, creating his own secular theology of purity, nationalism, and "positive Christianity."

Bonhoeffer was appalled by Hitler's blatant manipulation of the church. Bonhoeffer joined others who attempted to resist the influence of secular politics on biblical faith. He became one of the founding members of the Confessing Church, which aimed to preserve the light of biblical Christianity among the German people and eventually became the primary religious force of opposition to Hitler and the Nazis.

Bonhoeffer used his family connections to obtain a government position that kept him out of military service and allowed him to travel freely. Over time, however, Bonhoeffer felt his modest efforts to take a stand for the gospel against Nazism weren't enough.

This was his holy disturbance.

He had to do something more.

Through the sponsorship of a friend, Bonhoeffer joined the German intelligence organization called the *Abwehr,* an official "CIA" in Germany that nonetheless had been infiltrated by Allied spies and agents opposing Hitler. As part of one of these rogue groups within the Abwehr, Bonhoeffer served as the hub of a network of religious opposition. As bits of news emerged within the Abwehr regarding Nazi extermination of Jews and other atrocities, Bonhoeffer felt even more urgency.

It was time to take a stand.

He soon became a courier of information between agents who were concocting plans to assassinate Hitler. Essentially he was a double agent. He had the freedom to travel to other countries on official German intelligence business, but he actually passed along information among those seeking an end to Hitler's evil regime. Bonhoeffer even played a part in the July Plot, an attempt to assassinate Hitler.

Though he was not arrested at that time for his role in the assassination attempt, he was arrested for political reasons. He spent two years in prisons and concentration camps, where he spent his time writing. His book *The Cost of Discipleship* was penned during this time and has become a classic. In it he talks about "costly grace." He wrote, "It is costly because it costs a man his life, and it is grace because it gives a man the only true life."[1]

Those words were prophetic. After his role in the July Plot against Hitler was discovered, on April 9, 1945, Dietrich Bonhoeffer was executed by hanging in the Flossenbürg concentration camp.

Bonhoeffer gave his life to the message.

He died because he dared to take a stand.

THE COST OF COLLIDING WITH THE WORLD

If your life message is wrapped in the living gospel, I guarantee it will come to a collision point at some time in your life. You're bound for a head-on confrontation with the world.

You see, the world doesn't understand the gospel, and it struggles to embrace a life message based on it. In your quest to be the message, you will face difficulties, frustration, and seeming dead ends. You will, at times, be misunderstood. Your motives may be challenged. You may not have to face the evil of the Nazi regime, but there will always be those who want to discourage you from living out your life message. This becomes a direct challenge, a collision between your message and the world's values.

A Collision with Comfort (Will You Step Out of Your Comfort Zone?)

For one thing, the world will distract you with comfort. Lots of it. You and I live in the midst of extraordinary convenience and an abundance of plenty. We're way beyond appreciating the basic needs that are readily available—food, water, shelter—and we find ourselves assuming, even expecting, any number of creature comforts—a big TV, a favorite restaurant, a vacation trip.

Our version of hardship is when a car doesn't start or when our Internet signal is weak.

We all tend to find our personal comfort zones—those times and places and situations in life in which we can enjoy the deepest sense of relaxation and ease. There's nothing wrong with creating space in your life to relax and recharge. The danger lies in retreating to our comfort zones and setting up camp.

Once we're in a comfort zone, it's tempting to stay there. Once we sit down, it's hard to take a stand.

The problem occurs when we come to expect life to be easy for us. The problem occurs when we start protecting our comfort zones and ease of life, when that self-indulgence takes precedence over our life message of being the gospel to the world.

How tragic if we decline to make a difference in the world because we're just too lazy to bother.

A wealthy young man once asked Jesus what he must do to inherit eternal life. Jesus told him to obey the commandments. The young man replied that he had kept the commandments since childhood. Then Jesus said, "You still lack one thing. Sell everything you have and give to the poor, and you will have treasure in heaven. Then come, follow me."

The Bible tells us that the man went away sad because he was very rich (see Luke 18:18–23).

This story pointedly illustrates the problem of comfort zones. Jesus immediately homed in on the two things that the man counted on for security and comfort: religion and wealth. When Jesus asked the man if he had kept the commandments, Jesus knew that the man indeed had done so. The man knew all the right words and phrases and was well versed in the rituals of religion. In fact, he wrapped himself in religion as a security blanket.

The young man must have also found a lot of security in his wealth, because Jesus told him to give it away in order to be set free to follow Him.

But just as Jesus challenged him to move out of his comfort zone, He speaks to us. He says to you and me, "I am your security in life. Come, follow Me."

There are several other things that intrigue me about this story.

Why did the young man come to Christ in the first place? I think it must have been because he knew something was missing. Even though he had religion and wealth, he wasn't satisfied. I think that also applies to you and me. Sitting in our comfort zones, we may nonetheless sense that ease of life isn't enough, that something's missing. In some ways this parallels Bonhoeffer's story. He was born into a wealthy, prestigious family. And he was educated in the academic study of religion. But it wasn't enough.

I also think it's interesting that Jesus told the rich young man to sell everything and give the money to the poor. Giving to the poor meant identifying with the social outcasts in his community. We need to understand that in that day many believed wealth was an indication of God's favor and poverty was an indication of God's curse. The poor were outcasts for a reason, so it was thought. For Jesus to call this man to give his wealth to the poor was a radical statement. Jesus was challenging this assumption in the culture of that day, suggesting that the poor, being completely dependent on God, actually were closer to God than anyone else. Could it be our dependence on creature comforts might very well be an impediment to a deeper relationship with God?

But Jesus didn't call this man to devote his life to serving the poor. He told the man to give what he had to the poor but then to follow Him. And here is what I'm learning in my own life: the secret value of being pulled out of my comfort zone and being the message to others is how it deepens my personal relationship with God.

The act of stepping outside yourself, outside your level of comfort, opens up new areas of your heart and mind to the work of God. Acting on what you've heard from God reinforces your ability to hear from Him the next time.

Beyond that, obedience, even in the smallest way, moves you forward on the mission God has planned for you. A mission that will take you to places you never dreamed of and reveal things about yourself you never knew, some of them good and some of them not so good. Jesus's encounter with the rich young ruler gives us a glimpse of the challenges this life poses.

Christ calls you out of your comfort zone. He calls you to be the message of the gospel, and often the form that calling takes is helping others in the world. But ultimately it's about following Jesus. He wants you to rest in Him.

(Now, *there's* a comfort zone.)

Bonhoeffer wrote about the cost of discipleship. This is it. In all likelihood you will never face the threat of death for your faith, but God calls you to die to yourself, to jump out of your comfort zone and become the message to those around you. What He has for you—the person He wants you to be and the mission He has for your life—is greater than anything you could ever dream.

You can count on it. Your life message, one truly wrapped in the gospel, will have a head-on collision with a world that values comfort, ease, and security. For the rich young man, the cost was too high.

What about you?

A Collision with Apathy (Will You Get Involved?)

The world will conspire against you to keep you from getting involved. For one thing it will try to convince you that your one small life message doesn't matter. It will dress up apathy in the clothing of pragmatism and suggest that your efforts won't make a difference.

In Bonhoeffer's situation there must have been a lot of that. Hitler's regime was a juggernaut, seemingly unstoppable, certainly ruthless. It would have been easy for Bonhoeffer to think that his insignificant efforts wouldn't change anything. At the time it might have appeared that they didn't. Hitler wasn't assassinated, and Bonhoeffer was eventually executed.

But Bonhoeffer's *The Cost of Discipleship* has changed the lives of millions. His passion to shove a passionless church out of its comfort zone changed the course of German Protestantism. And his example and life message inspire people to this day.

Likewise, God may use your life message in ways you never expected.

Another thing the world does to distract you from living out your life message is to keep you endlessly, compulsively busy. Life with all its gadgets, devices, and technology drives us faster and faster in pursuit of more and more. We live a rat race—relentless, pressure filled, and complicated. One psychiatrist called it "a severe case of modern life."[2]

When we race through life, we have no margin, no time for anything else. No space for our life message to be lived out in the way God calls us to.

Now, look, we get it. We're like you. We have a family and four kids, and we're part of a big church. Any unscheduled part of our days is usually spent driving kids around, buying groceries, cleaning house, putting meals on the table, handling finances, and doing laundry.

Like you, little of what we do is just about us; it's about our families, our friends, our church. But with all of that, we are strapped for time.

So, yes, it's understandable. We have a lot to do every day.

But here's the problem. When we have no time and we have no margin in life, we will generally choose not to get involved in the things God is calling us to do. In our tiredness we will usually choose apathy over action. Our life message will be set aside, and we'll hop in the car to pick up more groceries.

Jesus told a parable that we've come to know as the story of the Good Samaritan. Jesus said,

> "A man was going down from Jerusalem to Jericho, when he was attacked by robbers. They stripped him of his clothes, beat him and went away, leaving him half dead. A priest happened to be going down the same road, and when he saw the man, he passed by on the other side. So too, a Levite, when he came to the place and saw him, passed by on the other side. But a Samaritan, as he traveled, came where the man was; and when he saw him, he took pity on him. He went to him and bandaged his wounds, pouring on oil and wine. Then he put the man on his own donkey, brought him to an inn and took care of him. The next day he took out two denarii and gave them to the innkeeper. 'Look after him,' he said, 'and when I return, I will reimburse you for any extra expense you may have.'
>
> "Which of these three do you think was a neighbor to the man who fell into the hands of robbers?"
>
> The expert in the law replied, "The one who had mercy on him."
>
> Jesus told him, "Go and do likewise." (Luke 10:30–37)

You may have heard the underlying story here. In that time and culture, Samaritans were looked down upon. They were considered the dregs of society. And so the meaning of the parable is very pointed: Jesus was saying that a priest and a Levite passed by the injured man, but the Samaritan, the lowest on the totem pole, was the one who lived out the gospel.

That's a powerful message. But as I read the parable again, I see another angle.

The priest and the Levite walked by and chose not to get involved. They "passed by on the other side" of the road. Perhaps they were busy. On their way somewhere. Out to buy groceries.

The other thing that pops out at me is that, for the Samaritan, stopping to help the injured man cost him a lot of time and money. He stopped, treated and bandaged the wounds, put the man on his donkey, and took him to an inn, where the Samaritan paid for a room in which the injured man could rest and recover. Presumably, he didn't get his grocery shopping done that day.

But he rescued a dying soul.

To be the message, you will have to consciously carve out time in your life. I know that's hard. But being the message always carries a cost. And part of that cost is intentionally protecting some corner of your life, fencing off some portion of time, for you to live out your message and be the gospel in the world. If your calendar and pocketbook are always overextended, you limit your ability to respond to God's prompting.

At first, that time you cordon off may sit there empty. Let it. That's okay. Use it as a time of quiet to listen to God. Make it an opportunity for a divine whisper. In time, that portion of your life will become more active in service and pursuit of your life message. Opportunities will emerge for you to be the message of the gospel to someone else. And soon you'll be looking to carve out more time from your life to get involved.

But I encourage you to endure the cost.

Otherwise, you'll simply "pass by on the other side."

A Collision with Fear (Will You Take a Stand?)

The world will try to frighten you away from living your life message.

Sometimes that fear will be in the form of doubt. Self-doubt. "I don't know what I'm doing." "I don't have the skills." "I don't think I can make it." "I'm not sure this will work."

Of all Jesus's disciples, Peter is the one I most identify with. He's the one who repeatedly faced doubt and fear—and repeatedly chickened out. He was the one who so eagerly stepped out of the boat to follow Jesus, who was walking on water. Then, when he looked down and saw how dangerous it was, his fear was bigger than his faith, and he started to sink (see Matthew 14:22–31).

Peter was also the one who, when asked by Jesus, "Who do you say I am?" confidently replied, "You are the Messiah, the Son of the living God" (Matthew 16:15–16). But then shortly afterward as Jesus was being tried, three times he denied knowing Christ out of fear for his own safety (see Luke 22:54–61).

But that's not the end of Peter's story. The Bible goes on to report that he becomes the leader of the early church. He is persecuted, imprisoned, and beaten, yet his commitment to the cause of Christ remains unwavering. He takes a stand, one that ultimately costs him his life.

I think you and I are probably like Peter. It may take us some time to develop the confidence and to overcome the fears we have as we live out the message of the gospel to the world.

Sometimes that fear might involve publicly taking a stand for Christ.

If there's a go-to story in the Bible about taking a stand and living one's life message, it has to be the story of Daniel, Shadrach, Meshach, and

Abednego. The "fiery furnace" is so familiar to us as a children's Bible story that I'm afraid we miss the meaning entirely.

Lean in close and listen.

The background is this: The army of Babylon, led by King Nebuchadnezzar, invaded Israel and captured its cities and towns. Most of the nation's valuables were carted back to Babylon as prizes of war. That loot included the brightest and best Israelite minds, among them Daniel, Shadrach, Meshach, and Abednego.

Rather than simply making these men slaves, Nebuchadnezzar educated them according to Babylonian customs, thought to be superior to all others in the world, and added these obviously brilliant young men to his cadre of advisors. At the time that group of wise men—an ancient version of what we might call a think tank or brain trust—was composed primarily of sorcerers and magicians.

These four Hebrews, however, proved to be quite different.

One night Nebuchadnezzar had a dream that greatly troubled him. He called his usual wise men to tell him what the dream meant, only this time he wanted them to tell him not just the interpretation but the dream as well.

When they could not do that, Nebuchadnezzar ordered all of them killed.

Facing execution, Daniel asked for more time so he and his three friends could pray. Then Daniel returned to the king and was able to tell him the dream itself, which involved a tall statue made of various materials, as well as the interpretation, which involved the fate of nations, many of which did not yet exist.

Overwhelmed by the accuracy of Daniel's account of the dream and elated at the interpretation, Nebuchadnezzar showered Daniel and his three friends with gifts. They all were appointed to high positions in government.

But then Nebuchadnezzar ordered his artisans to create a golden statue that resembled the one in his dream. When it was in place, he ordered everyone in his kingdom to bow down before the statue and worship it. Shadrach, Meshach, and Abednego refused to do so. They stepped out of their comfort zone and stood for their God. When Nebuchadnezzar learned of their refusal, he sentenced them to be executed by being thrown into a massive firepit.

As the three men stood before the king, they faced a defining moment: whether to bow to the golden image and remain physically alive but violate what they believed, or refuse to worship the image and remain faithful to God while facing certain physical death. Standing there quite literally between life and death, they said, "If we are thrown into the blazing furnace, the God we serve is able to deliver us from it, and he will deliver us from Your Majesty's hand. But even if he does not, we want you to know, Your Majesty, that we will not serve your gods or worship the image of gold you have set up" (Daniel 3:17–18).

Nebuchadnezzar had the men put into the furnace.

Shadrach, Meshach, and Abednego knew in their minds and believed in their hearts that God was always present. But they had never experienced His presence in such a real and vital way as they did when they were thrown into the furnace. The Bible tells us the three men were not touched by the fire. Looking in, Nebuchadnezzar observed this—and more. He asked his advisors, "'Weren't there three men that we tied up and threw into the fire?' They replied, 'Certainly, Your Majesty.' He said, 'Look! I see four men walking around in the fire, unbound and unharmed, and the fourth looks like a son of the gods'" (verses 24–25).

In saying that the fourth person looked like a "son of the gods," Nebuchadnezzar was more correct than he could have possibly known. That fourth person was not merely a son of the gods, but the Son of God—Jesus.

Of course, the three young men were pulled out of the fire. And the miracle was evident to all; their God had honored the life message of Shadrach, Meshach, and Abednego and had worked a miracle to save them.

Because these young men had taken a stand, Nebuchadnezzar turned his heart, and his kingdom, to God.

Try for a moment to put yourself in their shoes and imagine how those three young Hebrews must have felt in the seconds before they were placed in the fiery furnace. I imagine they expected to die a painful death. I also imagine their faith was so great that when they found they weren't being consumed by the fire, they weren't even surprised!

I wonder what was in Bonhoeffer's heart when he followed his holy disturbance and began his life of espionage. Did he, as a pastor-spy, wonder if someday he'd be caught and executed? Did he know bone-chilling fear? And what about the morning of his execution? Did his faith falter?

Well, in fact, history recorded some of the events of that day. The camp doctor, H. Fischer-Hüllstrung, was present with Bonhoeffer that morning. He wrote, "I saw Pastor Bonhoeffer kneeling on the floor, praying fervently to God...so certain that God heard his prayer.... I have hardly ever seen a man die so entirely submissive to the will of God."[3] As Eric Metaxas wrote in his excellent biography *Bonhoeffer: Pastor, Martyr, Prophet, Spy,* "Others testified that, up to his last day, the 39-year-old Bonhoeffer remained cheerful. He knew what he had to do, was reconciled to God's will, and was able to climb the steps to the gallows 'brave and composed.'"[4]

That's the kind of faith I want to have.

Our lives may never be on such a collision course with evil and death as Daniel and his friends or Dietrich Bonhoeffer, but their examples give encouragement to us who face lesser fears.

If our life message is challenging for us to carry out, can't we look at these and others who have faced death and believe that God can overcome our challenges?

When our life messages become diluted by comfort zones, apathy, and fear, don't these men and women of God speak to us about keeping our hearts focused on carrying out the life message God has for us?

CHAIN REACTION

We may never be called to face down an evil dictator or walk through fire, but we should not think that evil was limited to Hitler in the thirties and forties or that because Bonhoeffer lived in an unusual time, he had a rare opportunity to take a stand. Every generation has its own evils to face.

It's all too painfully familiar now, the extraordinary events of the tragic Columbine High School shooting. You no doubt have heard about two of the girls, Rachel Scott and Cassie Bernall, devout Christians who were shot in the high school that day. It was April 20, 1999. The shooters had specifically chosen that date because it was Hitler's birthday.

Evil spawns evil.

While certain details about what was said at the time of the shootings are in dispute, what's not questioned is that both girls were outspoken about their faith. And it's also verified that the two gunmen mocked these girls for their faith and targeted them because of it.

Sometimes the world confronts the gospel with force and seeks to eradicate it.

Cassie and Rachel died because, even at their young age, they had a life message that was wrapped in the gospel. That life message came to a collision point with evil. They had taken a stand, and it cost them their lives. Their courage puts a new perspective on what our life message can and should stand for.

A month before her death, Rachel Scott wrote in a school essay, "I have this theory that if one person can go out of their way to show compassion, then it will start a chain reaction of the same."

And that's the hope of the gospel—that you and I will take a stand and, in doing so, compel others to take a stand, starting a chain reaction.

Being the message is not about you changing the world on your own.

It's simply about you, in a special moment, taking a stand and letting God change the world.

LIFE SURRENDER

Several years ago I (Kerry) gave Chris a tandem bike for Christmas. She had told me for years that she thought it would be wonderful if we had a bicycle made for two. I think she romanticized how great it would be for us to sit on a bicycle together and pedal through the neighborhood on a sunny day. I kept telling her, "Honey, I don't think it sounds romantic at all. In fact, it sounds like a lot of work trying to pedal a bike that big."

I finally gave in and bought the bike, surprising her with it on Christmas morning. When she saw it, she went straight to the bike, pointed to the front seat, and said, "This is my seat." Then she put her hand on the rear seat and said, "And this is your seat."

At first I didn't think much of it because the seats looked exactly the same. But on our first tandem bike ride, I quickly discovered why she wanted the front seat. Only the person in the front seat can steer. The handlebars for the person on the backseat don't even move!

I also soon discovered that the person in the front seat has control of both the front and back brakes. So, in essence, Chris got to control where the bike went and when it would stop. I had no control over anything! All I could do was pedal.

I think I now know why she wanted that tandem bike so badly. It put her in total control!

Chris and I laugh about our rides on the tandem bike, but it's a great picture of what it means to follow Christ and daily surrender to His care and control. Christ demands the front seat in our lives. He steers and directs my life where He wants it to go. My only job is to sit on the backseat and stay connected to Him. I have to surrender to His control.

Many times, however, I take the front seat of my life. Right away I become filled with anxiety and fear, and I feel powerless to make it up the hills of life. It's a moment-by-moment surrender for me as I have to go back to the rear seat and return control to Christ.

Every day I have to remember to take the backseat and say, "Jesus, I need Your power today to love my family unselfishly because I so easily get self-centered. I need Your wisdom today to lead the church because I feel clueless about what to do next. I need Your strength today to break free from this destructive habit that's holding me back. I can't do it."

As I surrender to Christ, He fills me with His strength, wisdom, love, and self-discipline. All I have to do is sit on the backseat. And keep pedaling.

There's a poem I've had in my office drawer for years that means so much to me and speaks about this surrender to Christ.

At first, I saw God as my observer,
my judge,
keeping track of the things I did wrong,
so as to know whether I merited heaven
or hell when I die.
He was out there sort of like a president.
I recognized His picture when I saw it,
but I really didn't know Him.

But later on
when I met Christ,
it seemed as though life was rather like a bike ride,
but it was a tandem bike,
and I noticed that Christ
was in the back helping me pedal.

I don't know just when it was
that He suggested we change places,
but life has not been the same since.

When I had control,
I knew the way.
It was rather boring,
but predictable…

It was the shortest distance between two points.

But when He took the lead,
He knew delightful long cuts,
up mountains,
and through rocky places
at breakneck speeds,
it was all I could do to hang on!
Even though it looked like madness,
He said, "Pedal!"

I worried and was anxious
and asked,

"Where are You taking me?"
He laughed and didn't answer,
and I started to learn to trust.

I forgot my boring life
and entered into the adventure.
And when I'd say, "I'm scared,"
He'd lean back and touch my hand.

He took me to people with gifts that I needed,
gifts of healing,
acceptance
and joy.
They gave me gifts to take on my journey,
my Lord's and mine.

And we were off again.
He said, "Give the gifts away;
they're extra baggage, too much weight."
So I did,
to the people we met,
and I found that in giving I received,
and still our burden was light.

I did not trust Him,
at first,
in control of my life.
I thought He'd wreck it;
but He knows bike secrets,

knows how to make it bend to take sharp corners,
knows how to jump to clear high rocks,
knows how to fly to shorten scary passages.

And I am learning to shut up
and pedal
in the strangest places,
and I'm beginning to enjoy the view
and the cool breeze on my face
with my delightful constant companion, Jesus
Christ.

And when I'm sure I just can't do anymore,
He just smiles and says…"Pedal."
    —Anonymous

Ironically, the secret of your life message is letting go of your life. Giving up control of your brand and your image. Letting God do the steering, allowing Him to take you to those in the world who need your unique story to complete their own.

So what's your message?

And what are you waiting for?

Notes

Chapter 1: The Great Disconnect

1. Katy Pownall, "Uganda's Children Work on Dangerous Rock Pile," *USA Today*, June 1, 2008.
2. David Kinnaman, *unChristian: What a New Generation Really Thinks About Christianity...and Why It Matters* (Grand Rapids, MI: Baker Books, 2007), 29.
3. "Suffering Afflictions and Going the Second Mile," My Utmost for His Highest; Daily Devotionals by Oswald Chambers, July 14, 2013, http://utmost.org/suffering-afflictions-and-going-the-second-mile/.

Chapter 3: You Are the Gospel

1. David Platt, *Radical* (Colorado Springs, CO: Multnomah, 2010), 87–88.

Chapter 4: God's Megaphone

1. C. S. Lewis, *The Problem of Pain* (New York: Simon & Schuster, 1996), 83.

Chapter 5: From Mess to Message

1. Ryan Shook and Josh Shook, *Firsthand* (Colorado Springs, CO: WaterBrook, 2013), 53.
2. N. T. Wright, *The Challenge of Jesus: Rediscovering Who Jesus Was and Is* (Downers Grove, IL: InterVarsity Press, 1999), 184.

Chapter 6: The Power of Quiet

1. Andrew Murray, *Lord, Teach Us to Pray* (Philadelphia: Henry Altemus, 1896), 23.
2. Richard J. Foster, *Freedom of Simplicity: Finding Harmony in a Complex World* (New York: Harper, 1981), 132–33.
3. Richard J. Foster, *Celebration of Discipline: The Path to Spiritual Growth* (New York: Harper Collins, 1998), 20.
4. Brother Lawrence, *The Practice of the Presence of God* (Old Tappan, NJ: Fleming H. Revell, 1975), 17.
5. Bill Hybels, *The Power of a Whisper: Hearing God, Having the Guts to Respond* (Grand Rapids, MI: Zondervan, 2010), 17.

Chapter 7: Holy Disturbance

1. Stéphane Hessel, interview by Eleanor Beardsley, "World War II Survivor Stirs Literary World With 'Outrage,'" National Public Radio, September 22, 2011, www.npr.org/2011/09/22/140252484/wwii-survivor-stirs-literary-world-with-outrage.
2. Human trafficking is a global crisis, but most people who are trafficked in the US come from right here within our own borders. Teenagers between the ages of thirteen and seventeen are snatched from malls and other public places, drugged, and sent thousands of miles from home, where they are immediately forced to work as prostitutes. Scientifically accurate victim numbers don't exist—human trafficking by its nature makes counting trafficked persons all but impossible—but experts suggest that as many as sixty thousand people fall victim to human slavery every year. For a discussion of the problem, see Kevin Bales and Ron Soodalter, *The Slave Next Door: Human Trafficking and Slavery in America Today* (Oakland, CA: University of California Press, 2009).

3. Craig Groeschel, *It: How Churches and Leaders Can Get It and Keep It* (Grand Rapids, MI: Zondervan, 2008), 186.

Chapter 8: The Message the World Has No Explanation For

1. David Plotz, "Charles Colson: How a Watergate Crook Became America's Greatest Christian Conservative," *Slate,* March 10, 2000, www.slate.com/articles/news_and_politics/assessment/2000/03 /charles_colson.single.html.

2. Charles Colson, *Born Again* (Grand Rapids, MI: Chosen Books, 2008), 65.

3. Charles W. Colson, Good Reads, www.goodreads.com/author /quotes/27694.Charles_W_Colson.

4. Suzy Richardson, "Faith-Based Prison Ministries Leave Legacies of Transformation," *Charisma Magazine,* www.charismamag.com/spirit /devotionals/loving-god?view=article&id=1159:faith-based-prison -ministries-leave-legacies-of-transformation&catid=154.

5. Erin Koen, "A Mother's Love," She: True Stories Ordinary and Extraordinary, November 5, 2013, http://shetruestories.org/a-mothers -love/.

6. "Amish School Shooting," *LancasterPA.com* (blog), http://lancasterpa .com/amish/amish-school-shooting.

7. Bono, in Michka Assayas, *Bono: In Conversation with Michka Assayas* (New York: Riverhead, 2005), 203–4.

8. Amos 1:3–13 states that God would forgive Israel's enemies three times, so rabbis taught that forgiving more than three times was unnecessary.

Chapter 9: The Person the World Has No Explanation For

1. Tim Hansel, *Holy Sweat* (Nashville: W Publishing, 1987), 42.

2. John Stott, *Christ: Basic Christianity* (Downers Grove, IL: InterVarsity Press, 1994), 11.

3. Stott, *Christ,* 11.

4. Howard R. Macy, *Rhythms of the Inner Life: Yearning for Closeness with God* (Newberg, OR: Red Nose Fun, 2012), quoted in Ken Gire, *Relentless Pursuit: God's Love of Outsiders Including the Outsider in All of Us* (Bloomington, MN: Bethany, 2012), 81.

5. Philip Yancey, *The Jesus I Never Knew* (Grand Rapids, MI: Zondervan, 1995), 269.

Chapter 10: More Than Nothing

1. For a detailed account of Butchart's life, see Elias Butler and Tom Meyers, *Grand Obsession: Harvey Butchart and the Exploration of Grand Canyon* (Flagstaff, AZ: Puma, 2007).

Chapter 12: Take a Stand

1. Dietrich Bonhoeffer, *The Cost of Discipleship* (New York: Touchstone, 1959), 45.

2. "Coping with Your Crazy Busy Life," BeWell@Stanford, Stanford University, http://bewell.stanford.edu/crazy-busy.

3. Eric Metaxas, *Bonhoeffer: Pastor, Martyr, Prophet, Spy* (Nashville: Thomas Nelson, 2010), 237.

4. Metaxas, *Bonhoeffer,* 532.

TAKE THE
BE THE MESSAGE
CHALLENGE!

The Challenge is Simple: Speak Less – Love More

The Be the Message Church-Wide Challenge is a five-week campaign to ignite your church into a nation-wide movement to not just talk the talk, but walk the walk. Our kit will not only mobilize your congregation to live out a sermon and experience the love of Jesus Christ, it will help them grow deeper in their faith. The challenge curriculum includes a five-week small group DVD, a sermon series with illustrations, interactive guides, and additional downloadable resources.

BETHEMESSAGE.ORG

Continue your personal journey with Kerry and Chris Shook

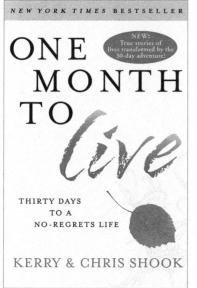

Discover the thirty-day process of learning to live passionately, love completely, learn humbly, and leave boldly. Make the most of your time on earth and live with no regrets.

Also Available:
- *One Month to Live Devotional Journal*
- *One Month to Live Guidebook*

Your relationships can go beyond Facebook and love-at-first-sight façades. Take the 30-Day Challenge for the adventure of a lifetime.

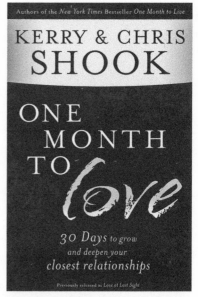

Previously released as *Love at Last Sight*.

Read an excerpt from these books and more at www.WaterBrookMultnomah.com.